BHAKTI YOGA

BHAKTI YOGA
THE PATH OF LOVE

Prabhuji

BHAKTI YOGA
THE PATH OF LOVE
BY PRABHUJI

First edition

Printed in India

Published by Prabhuji Mission
Website: prabhuji.net

Avadhutashram
PO Box 900
Cairo, NY, 12413
USA

Painting on the cover by Prabhuji:
"Classical letter colonial mail"
Watercolor on paper, New York
Paper size: 24" x 30"

Library of Congress Control Number: 2021906539
ISBN-13: 978-1-945894-28-2

Contents

ॐ अज्ञानतिमिरान्धस्य ज्ञानाञ्जनशलाकया ।
चक्षुरुन्मीलितं येन तस्मै श्रीगुरवे नमः ॥

oṁ ajñāna-timirāndhasya
jñānāñjana-śalākayā
cakṣur unmīlitaṁ yena
tasmai śrī-gurave namaḥ

Salutations unto that holy Guru who, applying the ointment [medicine] of [spiritual] knowledge, removes the darkness of ignorance of the blinded ones [unenlightened] and opens their eyes.

This book is dedicated, with deep gratitude and eternal respect, to the holy lotus feet of my beloved masters His Divine Grace Avadhūta Śrī Brahmānanda Bābājī Mahārāja (Guru Mahārāja) and His Divine Grace Bhakti-kavi Atulānanda Ācārya Mahārāja (Gurudeva).

Preface

The story of my life is nothing more than a long journey, from what I believed myself to be to what I truly am. It is an authentic inner and outer pilgrimage. It is a tale of transcending what is personal and universal, partial and total, illusory and real, apparent and true. My life is a flight beyond what is temporary and eternal, darkness and light, humanity and divinity. This story is not public but profoundly private and intimate.

Only what begins, ends; only what starts, finishes. One who lives in the present is neither born nor dies, because what has no beginning has no end.

I am a disciple of a seer, an enlightened being, and somebody who is nobody. I was initiated in my spiritual childhood by the moonlight. A seagull who loved flying more than anything else in life inspired me. In love with the impossible, I crossed the universe obsessed with a star. I have walked infinite paths, following the footsteps of those who could see.

Like the ocean that longs for water, I sought my home within my own house.

I am a simple intermediary who shares his experience

with others. I am not a guide, coach, teacher, instructor, educator, psychologist, enlightener, pedagogue, evangelist, rabbi, *posek halacha*, healer, therapist, satsangist, psychic, leader, medium, savior, or guru. I am only a traveler whom you can ask for directions. I will gladly show you a place where everything calms upon arrival, a place beyond the sun and the stars, beyond your desires and longings, beyond time and space, beyond concepts and conclusions, and beyond everything that you believe you are or imagine that you will be.

I am just a whim or perhaps a joke from the sky and the only mistake of my beloved spiritual masters.

Aware of the abyss that separates revelation and our works, we live in a frustrated attempt to faithfully express the mystery of the spirit.

I paint sighs, hopes, silences, aspirations, and melancholies, inner landscapes, and sunsets of the soul.

I am a painter of the indescribable, inexpressible, and indefinable of our depths. Or maybe I just write colors and paint words.

Since childhood, little windows of paper captivated my attention; through them, I visited places, met people, and made friends. Those tiny *maṇḍalas* were my true elementary school, high school, and college. Like skilled teachers, these *yantras* have guided me through contemplation, attention, concentration, observation, and meditation.

Like a physician studies the human body, or a lawyer studies laws, I have dedicated my entire life to the study of myself. I can say with certainty that I know what resides and lives in this heart.

It is not my intention to convince anyone of anything. I do not offer theology or philosophy, nor do I preach or teach, I simply think out loud. The echo of these words may lead you to the infinite space of peace, silence, love, existence, consciousness, and absolute bliss.

Do not search for me. Search for yourself. You do not need me or anyone else, because the only thing that really matters is you. What you yearn for lies within you, as what you are, here and now.

I am not a merchant of rehashed information, nor do I intend to do business with my spirituality. I do not teach beliefs or philosophies. I only speak about what I see and just share what I know.

Avoid fame, for true glory is not based on public opinion but on what you really are. What matters is not what others think of you, but your own appreciation of who you are.

Choose bliss over success, life over reputation, and wisdom over information. If you succeed, you will know not only admiration but also true envy. However, jealousy is mediocrity's tribute to talent and an open acceptance of one's own inferiority.

I advise you to fly freely and never be afraid of making mistakes. Learn the art of transforming your mistakes into lessons. Never blame others for your faults: remember that taking complete responsibility for your life is a sign of maturity. When you fly, you learn that what matters is not touching the sky but the courage to spread your wings. The higher you rise, the smaller and less significant the world looks. As you walk, sooner or later you will understand that every search begins and ends in you.

Your unconditional well-wisher,
Prabhuji

Introduction

Many speak about love, write emotional poems, and compose romantic songs. However, few actually love. Many embark on passionate affairs, get married, have children, and eventually get divorced, all without ever having truly loved.

Using people to ease the pain of loneliness, many seek to fulfill an inner void with another's embrace. Yet very few dare to set out on the adventure of discovering the profound mystery of the human heart.

Many people see love as a means of pleasure and expect to have the fortune of stumbling upon it. However, very few are interested in what love actually is.

The search for love does not usually arise from the desire to love, but from the need to be loved. Efforts are therefore focused on becoming worthy of love. This implies being attractive to another: men seek power, wealth, fame, and recognition; women embellish their physical appearance. For bhakti yogis, however, love is an art connected to the development and evolution of their own capacity to love. Thus, they dedicate their time and energy to mastering the skill of loving: first its theoretical aspects and then its practical ones.

Bhakti yoga is the yoga of love. Devotees aspire to a love different from the love in romance novels: it is not sentimental love that begins with sweet promises and ends in bitter disappointments, nor is it emotional love that arises from physiological processes and hormonal needs.

For bhakti yogis, love does not depend on an external relationship. Instead, it is a state of the soul. Far from being an interaction with another person, love is the perfume that emanates from our own presence, here and now. Bhakti is the purest and most elevated love. It arises from the depths of consciousness and the peace and silence of meditation. When we experience this love, we discover that it is not an emotion or a feeling, but what is *real* within us.

Because transcendental reality can only manifest itself in pure hearts, bhakti yoga offers a process of spiritual cleansing and purification. Although it is said that the path of bhakti is accessible to everyone, I would say that it is a journey exclusively for those who hear the call of love from the depths of their souls.

The message of bhakti yoga is unequivocal: love is the means and the goal. Without devotion, spiritual practice seems dry, prayer turns into unnecessary chatter, and religion becomes boring; it is reduced to a mere collection of laws, commandments, and ceremonies, and becomes more political than spiritual. Indeed, only by surrendering yourself to your own heart can you know what religion truly is.

Although bhakti is love of God, this path neither requires nor demands accepting divinity. Bhakti yogis do not preach about God, but about love. They posit that love is not only possible, it is the only option. At the same time, they consider any form of proselytizing unnecessary, since they know that the capacity to love is latent within us, and that the Divine becomes evident and obvious when love reveals itself.

Many believe that by devoting ourselves to God we will know his love. Bhakti, on the other hand, teaches us that only by surrendering to love will we know the Divine, because only when we offer our hearts can heaven take possession and make them its own.

Bhakti yoga states that our own hearts are the gateway to paradise. It invites us to pass through this door that is always open and leads to the beyond. Then, like sacred magic, grace will manifest itself in our lives, divinizing the ordinary.

The path of devotion reveals the paradise inherent in our daily routine. It shows us that the kingdom of heaven is not to be found in some unknown place—it is the closest thing to us. But we can only dwell in it after the revelation of our own divine nature.

Our preconceived ideas and concepts about love are a great obstacle to experiencing it, as we cannot love without transcending the mind. Pondering over love or trying to rationalize it is to lose it, since love is a state that transcends logic and goes beyond thought.

Bhakti yoga not only teaches us to love but also to systematically "go mad," as true reason resides in divine insanity. From this path's perspective, it is absurd to think we can understand love; the only sane thing is simply to love.

According to bhakti yoga, a master is not necessarily one who has great knowledge or can perform miracles, but is one who loves. Love, however, is not an endowment or privilege reserved for enlightened beings; it is a treasure that existence has placed within each and every one of us. In order to love, we should not wait to be saints. On the contrary, if we just love, we will become saints. Therefore, strive not for enlightenment, but for love… only by loving will we know who we really are.

To love is to live according to the law of life, which is love. When we live according to this law, we may not become rich or famous, but we will be blissful. Bhakti yoga is directed toward the experience of absolute bliss that helps us break the chains of worldly suffering. If attachment is our captivity, then love is the path to freedom.

Without love, we live in indifference and without meaning, treading a tedious path from the cradle to a cold grave. Only by experiencing love's warmth, light, magic, and mystery, will it be worthwhile to have lived.

If these words have awakened your curiosity about the mysterious melody called *love* that dwells within your heart, then I will consider my labor successful.

Chapter 1

What is bhakti?

he kṛṣṇa karuṇā-sindho
dīna-bandho jagat-pate
gopeśa gopikā-kānta
rādhā-kānta namo 'stu te

O Krishna, you are the ocean of compassion, the friend of those who are afflicted, and the Lord of the world. You are the master of the *gopas* (the cowherd boys) and the beloved Lord of the *gopīs* (the cowherd girls) [of Vrindavana]. O lover of Rādhārāṇī, salutations unto you.

(*Śrī-kṛṣṇa-praṇāma-śloka*)

The Sanskrit word *bhakti* stems from the root *bhaj*, meaning "to serve or to honor." Bhakti is "devotion to divinity." In the sacred Vedic scriptures, we find the following synonyms for bhakti: *prema*, *prīti*, *praṇaya*, *apahnava*, *rakti*, *anurakti*, *anurāga*, *niṣṭhā*, *āsakti*, *parāyaṇatā*, *abhiniveśa*, *saṁśraya*, and *upāsanā*.

Bhakti is a golden cord that firmly ties the devotee's heart to the lotus feet of the Lord; it is devotion to God with the sole aim of serving him.

In the *Śāṇḍilya Bhakti Sutra*, it is stated:

sā parānuraktir īśvare

> Supreme attachment to God (Īśvara) is called *bhakti*.
>
> (*Śāṇḍilya Bhakti Sutra*, 1.2)

In the *Nārada Bhakti Sutra*, we read:

pūjādiṣv anurāga iti pārāśaryaḥ

> Vyāsa, the son of Parāśara, says that bhakti is devotion that is expressed through puja and similar acts.
>
> (*Nārada Bhakti Sutra*, 16)

For Rāmānujācārya, devotion is not an ordinary feeling, but supreme love illuminated by the wisdom of God.

> *ataḥ sākṣātkāra-rūpā smṛtiḥ smaryamāṇātyartha-priyatvena svayam apy atyartha-priyo yasya, sa eva pareṇātmanā varaṇīyo bhavatīti tenaiva labhyate para ātmety uktaṁ bhavati, evaṁ rūpā dhruvānusmṛtir eva bhakti-śabdenābhidhīyata,upāsana-paryāyatvād bhakti-śabdasya.*

> Hence, those who are endowed with remembrance and distinguished by a character of direct realization (*sākṣātkāra*) are chosen by the Supreme Self and gain the Supreme Self. They are loved more than anybody because the one they remember is such. This type of constant remembrance is designated by the word *bhakti*, "devotion," which has the same meaning as *upāsanā* (close attendance, service, or worship).
> (*Śrī-bhāṣya* on the *Vedanta Sutra*, 1.1.1)

According to Madhvācārya, the importance of bhakti is unquestionable. In sutra 3.2.19 of his *bhāṣya*, "commentary," on the *Vedanta Sutra*, he observes that the authentic nature of the soul cannot fully manifest itself without bhakti. To support his words, Mādhvācārya quotes a verse from the scripture *Māṭhara-śruti*, most of which has been lost over time:

bhaktir evainaṁ nayati
bhaktir evainaṁ darśayati
bhakti-vaśaḥ puruṣo
bhaktir eva bhūyasī

> Bhakti leads the living entity to the Lord and enables the soul to see God. The Lord is controlled by bhakti. Bhakti is indeed the greatest thing of all.
> (Madhvācārya, *Brahma Sutra Bhāṣya*, 3.3.53)

Swami Rāmdās, the great luminary of *Sanātana-dharma*, wrote this about bhakti:

> Bhakti is an intense longing and love for God, which enables the aspirant to keep up a constant remembrance of him, thus purifying his emotions and elevating his thought to the consciousness of reality. Bhakti is the adoration of God, who dwells in his own heart and fills the universe, and the surrender of all his actions to him. Here a fit of renunciation seizes the aspirant: a mental recoil from the unrealities of life that had so long enthralled him. Through the exercise of an awakened intellect he now begins to discriminate the real from the unreal, the eternal from the non-eternal.
>
> (*The Divine Life*)

The soul experiences an irresistible attraction to the Divine like a needle attracted by a powerful magnet. Bhakti is thus an ardent, sincere, and loving dedication of the soul toward divinity. Bhakti and yoga, in reality, are synonymous, because they both aspire to reach a union. Wherever there is love, there will be the intention to become integrated in happiness and bliss.

The process of bhakti yoga is a so-called methodology that teaches us to love. However, love can never be a means to obtain anything other than love itself. Therefore, this path is both the means and the end. As was eloquently expressed by Swami Vivekānanda, the great disciple of

Rāmakṛṣṇa Paramahaṁsa, in his famous book, *Bhakti Yoga*, "Bhakti is the search for the Lord that begins, continues, and ends in love."

Bhakti yoga leaves aside concentration techniques. Those who love do not need a technique to focus attention on their beloved because even if they tried to resist, they would be unable to cease from thinking about their beloved. The bhakta requires no methods of dhyana, "meditation." It happens spontaneously, and simply consists in sitting down to love. Devotees come to love the Lord with all their hearts, all their souls, and all their might. Their minds naturally flow toward God until they finally merge with him.

In this process of devotional union, we open our hearts and make ourselves accessible, vulnerable, and defenseless, like the *gopīs*, naked before Lord Krishna on the banks of the sacred Yamuna River. Rather than teaching us how to attain God, the way of the heart prepares us to be possessed by him; it allows us to be taken by the Divine.

His Holiness Swami Śivānanda of Rishikesh said:

> Pure unselfish, divine devotion, *śuddha-prema*, is devotion for devotion's sake. There is not a bit of bargaining or expectation of anything here. This higher feeling is indescribable in words; it has to be sincerely experienced by the devotee. Bhakti is a sacred, higher emotion with sublime sentiments that unites the devotees with the Lord.

I received this wisdom from the disciple of His Holiness Swami Śivānanda, His Holiness Swami Viṣṇu Devānanda, who was an authority on hatha and raja yoga, and one of my most beloved *śikṣā-gurus*. When I was staying at the Sivananda Ashram in Canada, in August 1989, Swami Viṣṇu Devānanda stopped suddenly during one of our strolls, looked at me, and said, "Bhakti is not emotion, but devotion." I never forgot his words, although it took me some time to understand them.

Bhakti yoga is recommended for emotional people because it helps them differentiate between emotion and devotion, and to grasp the subtle distinction between the two. Such people move from one emotional upheaval to another. When they are in a difficult situation, they are submerged in sadness and despair; they become euphoric when expectations are satisfied. Their identification with the emotional plane creates conflicts that divide and torment, and thus hinder development.

Emotionalism can draw a person into chaotic states. When feelings are uncontrolled, they take unexpected directions and are expressed in actions unreflective of the person's true interests, aspirations, and longings for tranquility and well-being. It is a kind of addiction or emotional slavery that can lead to inner turmoil and even madness.

Unlike emotion, devotion possesses order. The devotional process is a path that reunites, integrates and unifies the emotions, and guides them toward the Absolute. Bhaktas withdraw their hearts from the mundane in order to direct and project it consciously toward God.

Any emotional phenomenon contains within it a certain amount of power that energizes us and impels us to act. The power of unbridled and unfocused emotion can have a very destructive influence on our lives, but when channeled, it can be used to make positive changes. In this way, bhakti leads us from the instinctive to the Divine by teaching us to wisely utilize this very power as an impulse and a driving force in our search for God.

Chapter 2

Love

Bhakti yoga is the yogic path of love that aspires to an inner alchemy of emotions; it does not suggest suppressing earthly feelings or nullifying them mechanically, but transcending them by developing the discernment between attachment and love.

Attachment is the expression of love through a limited and undeveloped instrument. Although attachment and love have the same essence, the former takes place on a level where we only seek our own benefit. Attachment is actually an attempt to exploit others for the sake of one's own enjoyment.

As long as we perceive ourselves as separate and disconnected entities, love will manifest itself in us as attachment. Love is bliss and beauty, but through the ego, it can only be partially expressed. Consequently, love not only loses its glow but also causes suffering.

The external expressions of love and attachment are quite similar. Those who are attached and those who truly love both feel a profound interest in their beloved. It is the same with those who operate animal protection organizations and slaughterhouses: they both care about animals, but with radically different intentions.

Attachment transforms us into dictators, hungry to control and dominate. Striving to possess everything, we even try to turn people into personal property. However, this world of names and forms is an ephemeral reality and a dynamic flow in constant transformation. Consequently, our yearning to possess inevitably dooms us to suffer.

In the end, we fall into the clutches of what we intend to control. We end up being manipulated by what we are trying to dominate; what we want to possess, in reality, possesses us. In trying to restrict the freedom of others, we lose our own.

Moreover, attachment to objects creates a kind of addiction that makes us dependent on them. Those who are attached erroneously believe that their happiness completely depends on the object of attachment. By assigning exaggerated value to temporary circumstances, they fall into an obsessive emotional state and become disconnected from reality.

All attachments are psychological illusions that block our sensitivity to others. This leads us to relate to people depending on the threat they pose or the help they offer in fulfilling our own ambitions. However, love is possible only if we transcend all types of attachment.

Attachment is a typical symptom of the ego phenomenon; the "I" is nothing more than an accumulation of attachments. Attachment is selfishness, while love is generosity. Attachment is self-love, while love is universal attachment. The ego lacks love, whereas love is free of ego.

To be attached is to desire to receive, while to love is also to be ready to give and share. The majority of people say they look for love, yet what they really crave is to be loved. Not finding love in themselves, they beg for it from others. But those who seek love from another person because of an inner void will always ask, demand, make claims, and, ultimately, get stuck in worldly attachment. As long as we do not find bliss within ourselves, we will continue to need others. On the contrary, love cascades from the hearts of beings who are full and complete, and who recognize themselves as love.

Attachment is a mere emotional experience, while love is existential. Worldly attachment disintegrates our inner peace. It leads us to conflict and even hatred. Love, on the contrary, is a deep longing to erase limits and to eradicate differences until becoming one with the Whole.

Attachment belongs to the dual and relative plane since it requires a relationship with another person; it is part of the subject–object phenomenon. On the other hand, love corresponds to the Self and belongs to the Absolute realm.

It is said that love is blind, but really, lack of sight is a symptom of attachment, which is the love of sleepwalkers. Love is attachment in full awareness. The more we love, the more conscious we become. The more intense our love, the clearer our vision.

Attachment is the love of the ego, love for the earthly. Love is the soul's attachment to the Divine; it is an enlightened being's attachment to God. Worldly love enslaves us, but divine love frees us. The former chains us to the mundane, the latter to the celestial. One tethers us to illusion, the other to reality.

Levels of love

Opinions on love are so varied that people often seem to be talking about different subjects. We are inundated with ideas and theories on love conveyed by newspapers, magazines, novels, the radio, television, and websites. However, it seems the more that is said about it, the less we understand.

It is so difficult to objectively state what love is because the definition of love is influenced by our perceptions. Just as a light bulb's brightness varies according to our distance from it, the experience of love's intensity depends on our position on the evolutionary ladder and how we identify with our different attributes. If we want to recognize from which level we love, we must observe our behaviour and attitudes.

Physical love

For someone at a basic level on the evolutionary ladder who identifies mainly with the physical body, love is a form of enjoyment or sensory pleasure. Such a person fits the description by Nicolas Sebastien Roch de Chamfort (1740-1794 CE), who said: "Love, as it exists in society, is not love, but the exchange of two fantasies and skin contact."

At this early stage of development, love manifests itself only as the release of certain chemical substances, as a physiological phenomenon. When only the corporal reality is perceived, love is closely identified with sexual appetites or lustful desire. In Sanskrit, the expression of love in its coarsest form is called *kama* or *kāmanā*, meaning "lust" or "desire."

We are also reduced to the physical plane if we only love *our people*, that is, those related in some way to our body, whether by blood or country.

Emotional love

Those who identify with their emotions believe that they feel love with the heart, but this type of love is simply mental activity.

The dramatic relationships portrayed in soap operas and romantic films, in which characters try to satisfy their own egoistical needs, are taken as models by emotional people. Their love is a mixture of cheap sentimentalism with adolescent whims. It is subject to change: a person can initially feel attracted to someone, fall madly in love, but later feel that the other has become not only unpleasant but even unbearable. And vice versa: someone who is intolerable now can become likeable and attractive in the future.

In the stage of attraction, a person feels in love, but the only certain thing is that he or she is attached. Rather than saying, "I will love you forever," they should say, "I am temporarily attached to you." Closer observation reveals that potential hatred lies within attachment: today we are attached and tomorrow we detest each other. Our friend today can become our enemy tomorrow and vice versa. Attachment is no more than another aspect of hatred: they are two sides of the same coin.

Intellectual love

For those who especially identify with their thoughts, love is experienced as an intellectual phenomenon. Intellect is the mental function of evaluating, judging, and discriminating. The love of this type of person generates expectations, such as the arrival of a so-called prince charming or dream girl.

In this way, many love from their imagination: they compose songs, write poems, or pen romantic novels. Their love is merely theoretical, rather than real and alive, because although they spend long periods of time thinking about love, they rarely love.

Intellectual lovers are calculating. Like businesspeople, they never give without receiving something in exchange. Incapable of loving unconditionally, they demand reciprocity and love only if it is returned. Consequently, if two such people meet, they will surely remain as empty-handed as before. Since both want to receive, neither will get anything and both will feel frustrated. They may share the same roof, but they will never live together. They may communicate, but will never reach communion.

Devotional love

As mentioned before, in the *Śāṇḍilya Bhakti Ṣutra* it is stated:

sā parānuraktir īśvare

Supreme attachment to God is called *bhakti*.
(*Śāṇḍilya Bhakti Sutra*, 1.2)

Bhakti is *parānurakti*, which means "an attachment to God or anything related to what is sacred." In the early stages, aspirants need to assign qualities to the Absolute so they can become attached to it. Since attachment belongs to the objective realm, devotional attachment requires symbols of the transcendental in the dual and relative reality. Hymns, books, temples, and deities are essential features for worldly attachment to become devotional. To the extent that the devotees become attached to God, they detach from the world. However, until the Absolute without qualities is reached, this experience will only be devotional attachment, not transcendental love.

There is a big difference between worldly attachment and attachment to God. The former brings about fear, confusion, suffering, and pain, while the latter bestows peace of mind and happiness. Selfish attachment turns into addiction and slavery; devotional attachment becomes divine love.

The path to love begins at our identification with body and mind, and ends in the experience of the spirit; it sets sail from the relative and disembarks upon the Absolute. It goes from man and arrives at God: to get attached is human and to love is divine.

God is love, and since we are an integral part of divinity, love is our nature, the very essence of who we are. Love is as vital to the soul as breath is to the body. Our innate need for love is proof that the divine spark dwells within us.

Directing our love to the world of names and forms is as futile as trying to quench our thirst by dipping our hands or feet in water. Only when we direct our love to its origin will it rain down upon everything and everyone. A beautiful verse illustrates this:

yathā taror mūla-niṣecanena
tṛpyanti tat-skandha-bhujopaśākhāḥ
prāṇopahārāç ca yathendriyāṇāṁ
tathaiva sarvārhaṇam acyutejyā

> By watering the roots of a tree, each and every one of its parts, from the trunk to the branches to the leaves, become filled with energy. When the stomach receives food, each and every sense and limb of the body is strengthened. In the same way, worship directed toward the everlasting Lord satisfies everyone.
>
> (*Bhāgavata Purana*, 4.31.14)

Only bhakti will satisfy us and simultaneously fill us with love for all, since all beings are the branches, flowers, and fruits of this immense tree of cosmic manifestation, whose roots are the divine Self.

Love is divine; it is *of* and *for* God, belonging and dedicated to the Self. As we advance on this path, we stop attaching ourselves to certain people because they serve our purposes, and we love the divinity that they really are. We begin to see an altar within all beings, upon which lies the divine presence.

Transcendental love

Bhakti yoga starts with selfish attachment, or love for the mundane; then, it goes through devotional attachment, which is love for God as a separate entity; finally, it culminates in transcendental love, where divisions between the lover and loved one vanish.

Before reaching transcendental love, there are still prayers, rituals, and a devotional relationship between devotees and the Lord. In the last stage, there is observation, and then only meditation remains.

As we move forward in the process of bhakti yoga, the pleasure offered by the dual plane becomes increasingly dull and our energy begins to flow toward the transcendental sphere. Sex, attachment, and even devotion imply a relationship between two people. On the other hand, transcendental love is not a meeting but a communion; it is not loving someone, but loving life, existence, and the Whole. Transcendental love lies beyond carnal desire, mental or emotional attachment, and even spiritual devotion. In that total and absolute union, ecstasy blossoms.

Only then does it become clear that love is not a feeling or an emotion, but is the need to return to the ocean that every drop carries within its core. Love is the thirst to reconnect to our origins, to reunify with our source, to return to ourselves. To love is to go back to the place we never left; it is to come home, to God.

Expansion of love

Love expresses itself at each and every step on the evolutionary ladder. Most people only move within private and personal territories. Due to their limited level of consciousness, they are only interested in themselves and their own needs. At this elementary stage of development, love excludes others and is personal, selfish, narrow, and sectarian. But as people evolve, their interests extend to their family, a kind of tribalism. They become concerned not only about themselves but also their partners, parents, children, and relatives. They feel the need to ensure not only their own well-being but also that of those physically closest to them.

As people develop further, they begin to notice the partiality of affection limited to family. At this point, their love extends toward the community and includes the need to express brotherly feelings toward their neighborhood or city. Many volunteer in community services, such as helping those in need or donating blood.

In the next stage, love expands even further and can manifest into a global cause such as defending human rights. These fraternal feelings bring the willingness to sacrifice for others. People at this stage are ready to defend others' rights. As this development continues, love extends to all, surpassing boundaries or borders, without differentiating gender, race, or religion.

Love for others is also expressed as compassion for living creatures. Vegetarianism is one of the highest expressions of an all-embracing love that upholds every living being's right to life. Our love is universal only when we renounce our complicity in the massacre of innocent animals for our personal gratification.

If we want humanity to have a better future, it is essential to allow our love to expand with an inclusive attitude. This does not imply losing interest in ourselves or self-negligence, nor renouncing affection for our family members, friends, or country. Rather, our capacity to love continues to expand to encompass all beings until no one and nothing is excluded. Universal love is the supreme quality that characterizes every enlightened being and saint, and is proof that God dwells in our hearts.

Egoistic love is like a light that illuminates only one closed-off room. Family love is like moonlight, which illuminates, but only partially and at a lower intensity. Love in its highest expression is tantamount to the radiance of the sun that brings light and warmth to everything and everyone without exception. Its superb clarity reaches and radiates light upon all, without making distinctions of any kind.

Similarly, egoistic attachment is like the water in our own glass that can quench only our thirst. Family attachment is like water from the well at your house, available solely for you and yours. Community attachment is river water that flows for everyone, including animals. Finally, the highest expression of love is like rain, falling and splashing on anything exposed to its freshness, without making any kind of distinction.

In summary, at the beginning of the bhakti path, we perceive ourselves only as a gross body and identify solely with our physical reality. Insofar as we become aware of more subtle levels of existence in an expansive movement, we transcend the limiting concepts of "I" and "mine." In this evolutionary process, carnal needs turn into worldly attachment, then devotion, and finally, into love.

Bhakti yoga is a process of expansion, which leads us from the limitations of our identification with a name and form to the experience of infinite consciousness without boundaries; it takes us from our personal awareness toward the universal.

This path presents the purifying magic of devotional service, which is the active and practical aspect of love. In human society, we generally work for remuneration. The usual motivation of our service is to receive enough money to maintain ourselves and our family. If something threatens us, we work out of fear, like prisoners. On the contrary, devotional service is motivated by attachment to God. When love awakens in us, our lives seem so ephemeral and tiny compared to the eternal that we naturally renounce the individual for the universal, the part for the Whole.

Bhakti yoga encompasses an expansive process that starts by establishing a devotional relationship with God. At the beginning, we experience attachment to the Lord and everything that is related to him. In these basic stages of bhakti, we unveil God in the periphery, recognizing him only in the place of worship.

Subsequently, the devotional process reveals the Absolute as the central axis of our existence. As we evolve, we get closer to God and discover him in the depths of everything and everyone. Only love reveals the Divine within us as our own reality.

Sublimation of love

Many consider the path of bhakti yoga to be a series of rituals and ceremonies. However, this liberating path implies a process that leads to a radical transformation from the basic levels of life up to existence in its purest state of consciousness.

Just as the same electrical source can switch on a light bulb, an air conditioner, or a large machine, the same love can reveal itself in physical, sentimental, intellectual, devotional, and transcendental ways. Sublimation lets us give love a new expression that naturally stops its flow in other directions.

Although sex and love share the same essence, when this energy is directed toward worldly needs and attachments our evolutionary process is inhibited, so we must elevate this energy. Since love cannot flourish from violent repression, bhakti yoga offers a conscious sublimation of the instinctive mind. Bhakti does not require blind or brutal repression on the physical or mental planes. It instead suggests that we open ourselves to the Divine and allow all of the energy to flow spontaneously to the depths of our being. Meditative sadhana facilitates the discovery of our divine dimension.

Just as a child gives up his toys as he gets older, bhaktas experience sublimation upon reaching certain spiritual maturity. Through a meditative process, they consciously direct emotions toward a specific deity. Placing their attention in the Lord makes them see earthly enjoyment as a weak shadow and worldly attachment as an empty reflection. The sweet nectar that stems from a relationship with God will become so superior to all worldly enjoyment, it will naturally lead them to the renunciation of all other pleasures, as stated in the Bhagavad Gita:

viṣayā vinivartante
nirāhārasya dehinaḥ
rasa-varjaṁ raso 'py asya
paraṁ dṛṣṭvā nivartate

> Sense objects withdraw from one who abstains from them, but the desire to enjoy them remains. However, when one becomes conscious of the Absolute, one ceases to experience attraction toward such objects.
>
> (Bhagavad Gita, 2.59)

If someone only eats onions for twenty years and then is offered a delicacy, the onions will be abandoned without hesitation; all previous appeal will vanish as if it had never existed. Likewise, when we are exposed to a new source of superior pleasure, all other attractions effortlessly wither away. Only then do we naturally lose interest in worldly enjoyment and perceive ecstasy.

Both ordinary and enlightened people experience love. For the former, it is a sentimental experience, while for the latter it is existential. The intensity and quality are so different that they seem to be utterly opposite experiences. Love for the jivanmukta, or one who is "liberated in life," stems not from any physical, mental, or sentimental level, but from meditation: from the depths of consciousness. When discovering love as our own essence, it expresses itself like a perfume emanating from our very presence.

The process of bhakti yoga consists of an authentic inner alchemy that can sanctify the human being. Like a philosopher's stone, bhakti divinizes the earthly, spiritualizes the material, and transforms our worldly attachments into true love.

Chapter 3

Devotion and desires

The value of human life is incalculable, but out of ignorance we squander our precious time, intelligence, energy, and attention, merely to satisfy desires. Our worldly whims impede the search for the door to the Divine. The less we strive to fulfill our desires, the more intense our attention to the sacred. As indicated in this verse:

samyaṅ-masṛṇita-svānto
mamatvātiśayāṅkitaḥ
bhāvaḥ sa eva sāndrātmā
budhaiḥ premā nigadyate

> A person is deeply attached to Krishna when the heart has become utterly tender, when is free of every worldly desire, and when the feelings of love have intensified. That purified emotion is known as *prema*, or "pure love."
>
> (*Bhakti-rasāmṛta-sindhu*, 1.4.1)

Our worldly appetites constitute serious impediments to directing our hearts to God. Rūpa Gosvāmī refers to this in his famous *Upadeśāmṛta*:

atyāhāraḥ prayāsaś ca
prajalpo niyamāgrahaḥ
jana-saṅgaś ca laulyaṁ ca
ṣaḍbhir bhaktir vinaśyati

When a person dedicates himself to the following six activities, his bhakti is destroyed: (1) overeating or accumulating more of anything than is required; (2) unduly striving in worldly matters; (3) having idle and worldly conversations; (4) being excessively attached to rules and regulations, or neglecting them; (5) associating with materially-minded people [who are not interested in spirituality]; (6) indulging in envy or greed.

(*Upadeśāmṛta,* 2)

Moreover, only those who have transcended the mind's demands and earthly appetites are capable of guiding others on the path of bhakti, as Rūpa Gosvāmī explains:

vāco vegaṁ manasaḥ krodha-vegaṁ
jihvā-vegam udaropastha-vegam
etān vegān yo viṣaheta dhīraḥ
sarvām apīmāṁ pṛthivīṁ sa śiṣyāt

> The wise who have transcended the impositions of the mind, the impulses of anger and speech, and the requirements of the tongue, stomach, and sexual organ can accept disciples in any part of the world.
>
> (*Upadeśāmṛta,* 1)

Those who understand that the cultivation of bhakti is made difficult by desires typically attempt to repress them. However, repression also comes from a desire: the desire not to desire. Consequently, repression only exacerbates the problem.

To transcend worldly desires, it is essential to understand their origin and nature: desire is a physical, mental, and emotional appetite characterized by an eager inclination toward attaining a particular enjoyment or pleasure.

According to the dictionary, the word *desire* comes from the Latin *desidium,* which means, "energetic movement of the will toward knowledge, possession, or enjoyment of a thing." To understand this term, we must delve into the meanings of *possession* and *enjoyment.* To *enjoy* means "to perceive or get pleasure from products and uses of a thing"; to *possess* means "to have a material thing with the aim of preserving it for oneself or for others." Desire is possessive par excellence; it is to have the ambition or appetite to own something in order to enjoy it.

Desire is part of a process that begins with *jñāna,* or "knowledge," which is mind, thought, past, and memory. Our knowledge is a collection of symbols: we receive information through the senses and we accumulate it in our mental warehouse as words, colors, textures, faces, places, scents, situations, sounds, melodies, and so on. We then encode this information as ideas, concepts and conclusions, and store it as symbols. All of these symbols produce certain sensations and feelings in us, either pleasant or unpleasant. From *jñāna, cikīrṣā* (desire) is born, which is the intention to have or repeat an agreeable experience, or to avoid an undesirable one. Desire is followed by *pravṛtti* (the will to act), then *ceṣṭā* (motor effect), and finally *kārya* (action).

Often, there is no relation between our desires and our needs. It is a fact that we do not always need what we want. A need is physical or biological; desire is psychological. Need is peripheral; desire is internal. Physiological appetites function to protect us, telling us when we must sleep, eat, drink, and so forth. Their aim is to maintain the body and preserve the species. They do not enslave us because they are needs that disappear once obtained: our thirst is quenched by drinking and hunger satisfied by eating. In contrast, desires do not disappear when the desired object is obtained, instead they strengthen and multiply. While failing to meet our basic needs can harm our health, liberating ourselves from our cravings and whims can be extremely healthy.

We might think that people wealthy enough to satisfy all of their desires would be able to be free of them. However, both the millionaire and the pauper suffer from the limitation imposed by their own cravings. The rich man has more possibilities to calm his anxiety, but being free does not mean owning a large cage, but rather having no need to leave it. In the Bhagavad Gita we read:

vihāya kāmān yaḥ sarvān
pumāṁś carati niḥspṛhaḥ
nirmamo nirahaṅkāraḥ
sa śāntim adhigacchati

> Those who have abandoned all desires, renounced all sense of possession, and lives detached and divested of ego attains true peace.
>
> (Bhagavad Gita, 2.71)

Being poor is not a lack of money, but an abundance of appetites. Being rich is not to have plenty of possessions, but the absence of desires. Real satisfaction is not achieved by repressing desires but by experiencing our transcendental nature, which is free from all worldly desires.

Desires and the present

Desires arise from the known, from the familiar, from the past, and they promise satisfaction in the future. To desire is to expect to repeat what has already been experienced. Under the dominion of desire, we are no different from it, and therefore, we become the past and the future. In this way, we move away from the now, the present, and ultimately, reality.

Under the control of the mind's demands, we are not alive, but merely prepare to live. As slaves of desire, we harbor hopes of one day reaching happiness, peace, and love. Desire becomes our lifestyle. We do not live in the present, but in constant expectation, and we interact with the present only as a means to get to the future, which is the only thing that we consider important and valuable. We feed the illusion of feeling fulfilled when we obtain coveted circumstances, people, or things. Ultimately, once enslaved by desires, we remain dissatisfied, because the future—as promising as it may be—cannot relieve the loneliness, fear, and uneasiness of the present.

Desires do not disappear if we repress them, nor can they ever be entirely satisfied. However, since desires need time to survive, and the present is timeless, they vanish effortlessly when we are in the moment. Living in the now, our desires vanish as if by magic.

Only in the present will you become aware that you alone are responsible for your suffering. This present moment can teach you that if you do not find satisfaction here, you will not find it anywhere, and that if happiness is here, it is everywhere. Transcending desire does not mean repressing it, but transforming the present moment into your entire life. Then you will experience that nothing is missing, and you will feel deep gratitude. In the now, life, existence, reality, and that emptiness that is so full of everything dwell.

Longing for God

Love for God keeps devotees focused on the Divine and does not let them direct their senses toward so-called mundane and bodily enjoyment. Just as a husband and wife are mutually consecrated in body and soul, devotees are consecrated to their beloved Lord in a divine romance, and they renounce any impulse to satisfy their own mental demands.

Bhaktas' attraction to the beauty of the Lord leads them to experience the elevated devotional state of *madana-mahā-bhāva*, or "pure and ecstatic intoxicating devotion for God." Devotees' energy, devoid of expectations, flows toward the Divine. Only the holy presence of Krishna calms the anxiety of the cowherd girls of Vrindavana, and he reciprocated their devotion.

The true sublimation suggested by bhakti yoga lies in transforming our desires into longings and converting our worldly appetites into longing for God, expressed as the aspiration for absolute freedom, infinite love, and unlimited expansion.

Longing is different from desire. While desire is directed at objects, longing is directed at the subject. When desirous, we seek to possess and accumulate externally, while longing produces an opening to our interior. To desire someone is not the same as to long for his or her company or association, because desire distracts us and prevents us from being truly present. Desire seeks to possess something, while longing aspires to *be*. Desire gives birth to worldly attachment, while longing nurtures devotion.

Desire is illogical, ridiculous, and irrational: it is like an ant that dreams of being an elephant, or a donkey that wants to be a lion. Longing is that of the silkworm to become a butterfly, or of the bud to blossom into a flower. Desire is capricious because it belongs to the world of the mind, while only the heart can truly long.

Desire is dangerous, violent, and ugly; longing is beautiful and harmonious. Desire is rajasic; longing is sattvic. We desire things like cars and money; we long for God. Desire binds, enslaves, and creates addiction, but longing frees. Desire leads to frustration and longing to peace. While desire may bring us enjoyment, happiness, and pleasure; longing leads us to bliss.

Need is of the body; desire, of the mind; longing, of the spirit. By igniting our longing for God, we appease desires for the world. *Bhaktas* surrender themselves to this longing, and let themselves be carried away by its flow. Longing for God is not ours; it is the sky longing for us. It is not the human being looking for God, but the divine call in the depths of the heart.

Chapter 4

God

In order to advance on the path of bhakti yoga, it is essential to understand the concept of God in the context of *Sanātana-dharma*. A lucid perception of the Hindu word *God* will allow us to move beyond the basic and elementary steps.

There are many Westerners who adopt Hinduism and inadvertently retain their previous theologies such as Judaism, Christianity, or Islam. However, because of significant differences, one who views the Eastern attitude through the lens of a Semitic cultural background will be unable to grasp the Hindu concept of divinity.

God

Nirguṇa-brahman

According to the *Viśva-dharma* religion, Brahman is the Absolute, the single and unchanging reality that underlies the manifold changing world. The sacred scriptures define Brahman as *sac-cid-ānanda*, "absolute existence, consciousness, and bliss."

The Upanishads refer to Brahman as the reality that transcends time and space, cause and effect, and good and evil; it is the pure and infinite consciousness beyond thought and mind. The *Aitareya Upanishad* states:

prajñānaṁ brahma

Consciousness is Brahman.
(*Aitareya Upanishad*, 3.1.3)

Similarly, the *Taittirīya Upanishad* states:

satyaṁ jñānam anantaṁ brahma

Brahman is truth, wisdom, and infinity.
(*Taittirīya Upanishad*, 2.1.1)

Brahman is the ultimate reality, or *satya*; the essence of wisdom, or jnana, and its nature is infinite, or *ananta*. In short, Brahman is the consciousness that illuminates everything.

Nirguṇa-brahman refers to its aspect that is devoid of attributes and formless, or *nirākāra*. Therefore, Brahman is described in jnana yoga solely through the path of negation: *neti-neti*, "not this, not this." We may hear many intellectual explanations, but we can only come to know Brahman through a direct, existential experience.

Brahman manifests an apparent reality through its own illusory power called *maya*, covers pure consciousness through *āvaraṇa-śakti* (covering power), and projects the dual world through *vikṣepa-śakti* (projecting power).

Saguṇa-brahman

Saguṇa-brahman, "God with qualities" is the view of the Divine from the human, the Absolute discerned by relative sight, and the apprehension of God from our dual platform of space and time and subject and object.

According to Sankya philosophy, purusha corresponds to Nirguṇa-brahman while prakriti is manifested reality. Therefore, Saguṇa-brahman, or Īśvara, is the descent of Brahman into the manifested. Saguṇa-brahman is the aspect responsible for the creation, maintenance and dissolution of the manifestation, which unfolds from Brahman as a cosmic dream. The following verse relates to God not as a creator, but as a magician, because the existence of the universe is illusionary.

ya eko jālavān īśata īśanībhiḥ
sarvāṁ llokān īśata īśanībhiḥ
ya evaika udbhave sambhave ca
ya etad vidur-amṛtās te bhavanti

> The One absolute, impersonal Self, who is a magician, appears as the Lord, the personal God, endowed with manifold glories. By its divine power, it holds dominion over all the worlds. At the times of creation and dissolution of the universe, the Self alone exists. Those who realize this become immortal.
>
> (*Śvetāśvatara Upanishad*, 3.1)

Īśvara means "the supreme controller of nature" and is the personal aspect of the Supreme Being. He is the omnipotent, omniscient, and omnipresent God.

eko hi rudro na dvitīyāya tasthur-
ya imāṁ llokān īśata īśanībhiḥ
pratyaṅ janāṁs tiṣṭhati sañcukocānta-kāle
saṁsṛjya viśvā bhuvanāni gopāḥ

> Since Rudra (Īśvara) exists, those who know Brahman see no reason to recognize any other deity. Rudra is the one who controls all the worlds with his powers. He is the innermost being in everyone. He creates this universe, maintains it, and ultimately destroys it.
>
> (*Śvetāśvatara Upanishad*, 3.2)

The knowledge of Īśvara brings with it the realization of the Absolute. Ultimately, Brahman hides behind the personal God. Īśvara emanates from Brahman from the first moment of creation and remains until its dissolution; he controls all that happens within the cosmic manifestation through maya, his universal power.

"Does a God exist who is the creator of this universe?" Religious people often ask this question. In Hinduism, faith in an almighty being is not an essential condition for followers, since God persists only as long as we consider ourselves separate entities from the cosmic manifestation. When we objectify the universe, we need an entity to have created it. Consequently, to the same degree that we and the universe are real, the creator will be real as well.

Within relative reality, we can only recognize objects that are localized in a specific time and place, and possess a particular name and form. Īśvara is Brahman endowed with qualities, the Absolute perceived from the dual structure, from within the *upādhis*, "limitations," of the mind: space, time, name, and form.

Īśvara is Brahman empowered with certain qualities that, though they may seem restrictive, enhance him. While a fish cannot survive out of water because of its physical characteristics, a scuba diver gets equipped with whatever is needed to dive beneath the sea and explore aquatic life. In the same way, just as a person extends the range of human capacities by wearing a diving suit, Brahman acquires qualities that do not limit its possibilities, but expand them.

Swami Śivānanda, in his very famous work, *Lord Krishna, His Līlās and Teachings*, explains the following:

> Though Lord Krishna [Īśvara] appeared in a human form, he had a divine body, or *aprākṛtika*. He was not born. He did not die. He appeared and disappeared through his Yoga Maya. This is a secret known only to his devotees, yogis, and sages.

Although Īśvara possesses qualities, these do not affect him, as Patañjali points out:

kleśa-karma-vipākāśayair
aparāmṛṣṭaḥ puruṣa-viśeṣa-īśvaraḥ

Īśvara is a distinct supreme soul, unaffected by afflictions (*kleśa*), works (karma), results (*vipāka*), and dormant karmic impressions (*āśaya*).

(*Yoga Sutra*, 1.24)

Īśvara is completely free and undisturbed by the results of the five *kleśas*, "afflictions": ignorance (*avidya*), egoism (*asmitā*), attraction or desire (*rāga*), aversion (*dveṣa*), and attachment to life (*abhiniveśa*).

The Lord transcends *vipāka*, "the results" of karma, or in other words, the results of actions motivated by the desire to obtain birth within a particular social class (*jāti*), longevity (*āyus*), and enjoyment or pleasure (*bhoga*).

Saguṇa-brahman is also *akarman*, "free of karma," because he is not affected by the three types of karma: negative, positive, and mixed. Likewise, he is beyond the *āśaya*, "karmic impressions, lying as seeds" in the subconscious mind (*citta*), which will be expressed as karmic results at a specific time.

Even though modern physics has shown that the world is not actually as it is perceived by the senses, our relative reality still appears to be made up of objects. In the same way, even though Brahman is beyond all qualities, as long as our perception of reality remains limited to the subject-object cognitive state, we must give Brahman attributes in order to perceive it. Īśvara is the Absolute in a form we can conceive within our dual and relative reality, the Divine observed from the human, the transcendental glimpsed from the mortal.

Bhagavān

Īśvara denotes the personal God, the controller of everyone and everything, while Bhagavān refers to his divine presence. If the title *Bhagavān* has been given to certain enlightened masters, such as Bhagavān Ramaṇa Maharishi, it is not because they are considered to be Īśvara—the creator, controller, dominator of the world—rather it is because the *presence* of the Divine, or Bhagavān, dwells within them.

The sage Parāśara, the father of Vyāsadeva, refers to Bhagavān as the total expression of all six qualities:

aiśvaryasya samagrasya
vīryasya yaśasaś śṛyaḥ
jñāna-vairāgyayoś caiva
ṣaṇṇāṁ bhaga itīṅgaṇā

> Complete power, wealth, beauty, fame, wisdom, and renunciation are the six qualities that are called *bhaga* (and the Lord is called *Bhagavān* for being endowed with them).
>
> (*Viṣṇu Purana*, 6.5.74)

Power: There is no greater power than the Self, because its power is exerted not from the external, but from the very roots of existence.

Fame: Divine fame is different from worldly fame because it transcends time. But even on the earthly plane, in one way or another, every human being has thought, heard, or spoken about God. Other civilizations mention him in the Torah, New Testament, Koran, and Zend Avesta. Some believers worship him in churches, others in mosques or synagogues. Although the names vary, wherever we go we will always find some notion of God.

Wealth: We all believe that we possess something. In reality, however, the owner of everything, including ourselves, is Bhagavān. It may seem that we possess consciousness, but it is consciousness that possesses us.

Beauty: Beauty is not a characteristic of something or someone, but the presence of Bhagavān. Beauty itself does not dwell in the object, but is in the eye of the beholder. It is not the beauty of our beloved that awakens our love; rather our love reveals to us our beloved's beauty. Only after discovering the divine presence of Bhagavān within will we delight in the authentic beauty that dwells within everything and everyone.

Wisdom: Only Bhagavān is able to know directly and without intermediaries.

Renunciation: We are slaves to whatever we cannot relinquish. Bhagavān's opulence is absolute because he is able to renounce it.

Bhakti yoga creates favorable conditions that allow us to perceive Bhagavān, the divine presence. Through worship, devotion will blossom. When we love Bhagavān, he is revealed as our own presence, the presence of what we really are.

The souls

Atman, "the universal and individual soul"

The *Aṣṭāvakra Gītā* refers to Atman in the following way:

ātmā sākṣī vibhuḥ pūrṇa
eko muktaś cid akriyāḥ
asaṅgo niḥspṛhaḥ śānto
bhramāt saṁsāravān iva

> Atman is the witness, all-pervasive, full, one, liberated, conscious, independent peaceful, and without action or desire. Due to delusion, Atman appears to belong to the world.
>
> (*Aṣṭāvakra Gītā*, 1.12)

The term *ātman* denotes "spiritual essence" or "soul." Atman is Brahman's intrinsic incarnation and dwells within every living creature; it is reality as individuality.

Atman is the reflection of the one Brahman in each and every one of us. In order to understand this, imagine for a moment the sun's reflections in many pools of water after a rain shower. Now suppose that one of these reflections begins to observe, explore, inquire within, and aspires to know its origin. First, it will discover its resemblance to the sun, but eventually it will awaken to the reality that the same sun is being reflected in each and every pool.

Atman is the Self, pure consciousness, the spirit in its universal and individual sense, beyond identification with the phenomenal world. Atman is the eternal, infinite and absolute within this temporal, finite, and relative reality. Like a hole in a sheet of paper that is not made of paper yet resides within it, Atman is a point in the form but utterly transcendental to it. It is the real based on the apparent.

Atman is Brahman dwelling in the living being; thus, when we experience Atman we will also recognize the eternal reality lying behind every name and form.

Jiva, "the living entity"

The term *jīva* stems from the Sanskrit root *jīv*, "to live," and refers to the eternal essence within every living being. Jiva or *jīvātman* refer to this very same Atman confined within a particular form, subject to samsara, "the repeating wheel of birth and death." It refers to any living being limited by a mind shrouded in *avidya* (ignorance), *mala* (impurity), and *vikṣepa* (distraction).

Since the true identity of the jiva is Atman, its essence is Brahman, as is detailed in the *Śvetāśvatara Upanishad*:

viśvataś-cakṣur uta viśvato-mukho
viśvato-bāhur uta viśvatas-pāt
saṁ bāhubhyāṁ dhamati saṁpatatrair
dyāvā-bhūmī janayan deva ekaḥ

> All eyes are his eyes, all faces are his faces, all hands are his hands, and all feet are his feet. The same God created the heavens and the earth, and then added two hands to a human being and two wings to a bird.
>
> (*Śvetāśvatara Upanishad*, 3.3)

This is also confirmed by the Bhagavad Gita:

sarvataḥ-pāṇi-pādaṁ tat
sarvato-'kṣi-śiro-mukham
sarvataḥ-śrutimal loke
sarvam āvṛtya tiṣṭhati

> He is the one whose hands and feet are everywhere; whose eyes, ears, and mouths dwell in all living creatures; and who surrounds all of them.
>
> (Bhagavad Gita, 13.14)

Just as on the cosmic plane, Īśvara is Brahman associated with maya; on the individual plane, jiva (subjective ego) is Atman covered by *avidya* (ignorance).

satyaṁ jñānam anantaṁ yad
brahma tad vastu tasya tat
īśvaratvaṁ tu jīvatvam
upādhi-dvaya-kalpitam

> Brahman is existence, wisdom, and the infinite. Īśvara, the omniscient Lord of the world, and the

individual soul are superimposed on Brahman through the two illusory attributes, maya and *avidya*, respectively.

(*Pañca-daśī*, 3.37)

sattva-śuddhy-aviśuddhibhyāṁ
māyāvidye ca te mate
māyā-bimbo vaśī-kṛtya
tāṁ syāt sarva-jña īśvaraḥ

There are two types of prakriti. When pure sattva predominates (unperturbed by other gunas), it is called *maya*. When impure sattva predominates (perturbed by other gunas), it is called *avidya*.

(*Pañca-daśī*, 1.16)

avidyā-vaśagas tv anyas
tad vaicitryād anekadhā
sā kāraṇa-śarīraṁ syāt
prājñas tatrābhimānavān

The [different proportions of the] admixture of *rajas* and tamas with sattva on which Brahman has cast its reflection gives rise to the different gradations of living entities [such as devas, men, and lower animals] who are subservient to *avidya* (nescience). This *avidya* is also called *kāraṇa-śarīra*, "causal body." When the individual soul identifies itself with this causal body, it is called *prājña*.

(*Pañca-daśī*, 1.17)

Unlike the jiva, which is dominated by *avidya*, Īśvara is not subject to the power of maya, but is its Lord. While the universal soul is referred to as purusha, the individual soul is called *viśeṣa-puruṣa*, "the particular soul."

Just as the ocean is the sum of all of its waves, Īśvara, "the Supreme Individuality," comprises all jivas. Just as the ocean cannot exist without waves, Īśvara cannot exist without jivas, and vice versa; they are interdependent.

Just as a wave has its own form, although it is composed of the ocean itself, the jiva has its own individuality within Īśvara, even though the essence of both remains Brahman, the One without a second.

The cosmic manifestation

In the *Chāndogya Upanishad* (6.2.2), it is said that Brahman is *ekam evādvitīyam*, "One without a second," who manifests this world of names and forms of his own free will. Brahman assumes a subject-object nature through the creation of an illusionary duality that allows self-observation, as Ādi Śaṅkara explains:

bījasyāntar ivāṅkuro jagad idaṁ
prāṅ nirvikalpaṁ punaḥ
māyā-kalpita-deśa-kāla-kalanā
vaicitrya-citrī-kṛtam
māyāvīva vijṛmbhayaty api mahā-
yogīva yaḥ svecchayā
tasmai śrī-guru-mūrtaye nama idaṁ
śrī-dakṣiṇā-mūrtaye

> Just like a juggler or a great yogi, he manifested solely of his own free will in this universe, which before creation had remained in an unmanifested state, like the potential tree within a seed. He then projected himself to become the endlessly varied world, due to the delusory play of time and space, both products of maya. This prostration is for the divine teacher Sri Dakṣiṇāmūrti.
>
> (*Śrī-dakṣiṇāmūrti Stotra*, 2)

All manifestation originates solely from Brahman because his own reality is all that exists. Therefore, the creation can only be Brahman. What we call *the world* is merely the apparent evolution of Brahman, as noted in the *Vedanta Sutra* and also in the *Bhāgavata Purana* (1.1.1):

oṁ janmādy asya yataḥ

> Om [Brahman is that] from which proceeds the creation, preservation and destruction of this [manifestation].
>
> (*Vedanta Sutra*, 1.1.2)

In order to manifest himself, Brahman assumes a dual male-female nature, in which the male aspect is called *purusha* and the female prakriti or shakti. The entire cosmic creation is composed of matter and spirit. Prakriti is "matter,"meaning, everything that is found to be subject to change. Purusha, on the other hand, is the "spiritual, eternal, and unchanging aspect." *Vidyā*, "wisdom," means correct discrimination between purusha and prakriti.

Just as a movie screen remains undamaged by the projection of a war film's exploding bombs, Brahman remains unchanged, despite the projection of the universe upon it.

In the Bhagavad Gita, Krishna refers to prakriti in the following way:

bhūmir āpo 'nalo vāyuḥ
khaṁ mano buddhir eva ca
ahaṅkāra itīyaṁ me
bhinnā prakṛtir aṣṭadhā

> Earth, water, fire, air, space, mind, intellect, and ego are the eight categories of my prakriti.
>
> (Bhagavad Gita, 7.4)

apareyam itas tv anyāṁ
prakṛtiṁ viddhi me parām
jīva-bhūtāṁ mahā-bāho
yayedaṁ dhāryate jagat

> This is my lower prakriti. Distinguish from it, O you of powerful arms! Know my higher prakriti, which adopts the form of jiva, by which the universe is sustained.
>
> (Bhagavad Gita, 7.5)

Through the three modalities of material nature called *sattva* (goodness), *rajas* (passion), and tamas (inertia), prakriti gives rise to illusion and ignorance, as noted by Swami Vidyāraṇya:

cid-ānanda-maya-brahma-
pratibimba-samanvitā
tamo-rajaḥ-sattva-guṇā
prakṛtir dvi-vidhā ca sā

The primordial substance is called *prakriti*, and is composed of three elements called *sattva*, *rajas*, and *tamas*. Brahman, which is pure consciousness and bliss, is always reflected in it. Prakriti is of two kinds [maya and avidya].

(*Pañca-daśī*, 1.15)

One of the essential differences between maya and avidya is that sattva predominates in the former, whereas *rajas* prevails in the latter.

If we pay attention, we notice that although we consider the world to be solid, real, and genuine, its existence is actually illusory. For something to be real, it must be continuous and permanent. A dream is clearly unreal because it has a beginning and an end. For example, we may dream we are millionaires but upon waking we realize that we are not: dreams lack continuity. In this regard, the *Yoga-vāsiṣṭha-sāra-saṅgraha* states:

jagat tvam aham ity ādir
mithyātmā dṛśyam ucyate
yāvad-etat sambhavati
tāvan-mokṣo na vidyate

> The world, you, me, etc., constituting illusory entities, are called *the visible*. Liberation is impossible as long as this illusion persists.
>
> (*Yoga-vāsiṣṭha-sāra-saṅgraha*, 3.3)

The verse says that, in fact, all that is "visible" is illusory, lacks absolute existence, and vanishes moment by moment. It is very difficult to notice the constant change that the world is undergoing, just as while watching a candle, we do not perceive how the fire consumes it. Only after a lapse of time can we see the change, in the same way that the candle, the entire world including us, is in flames. When we perceive the transience of life, we will begin to question whether we truly exist.

Creation manifests itself through the apparent evolution of Brahman from subtle to solid, from simple to complex, from unity to diversity. Brahman does not create from nothing, rather, it manifests from itself. During the process of involution, the temporal manifestation dissolves and returns to its eternal source.

The worship of Īśvara

The realization of Nirguṇa-brahman is the ultimate purpose of life. To be absorbed in the Absolute is the highest state. However, due to the mind's outward nature, it cannot focus on something it is unable to perceive. Since the mind can only conceive the tangible and concrete, the worship of Saguṇa-brahman, or Īśvara, is essential, at least in the beginning. This subject is clarified by Lord Krishna:

kleśo 'dhikataras teṣām
avyaktāsakta-cetasām
avyaktā hi gatir duḥkhaṁ
dehavadbhir avāpyate

The difficulty is great for those whose minds are occupied with the unmanifested, because it is very difficult for incarnated beings to achieve a goal that is not manifested.

(Bhagavad Gita, 12.5)

Puranic literature refers to Brahman as Īśvara in a trinity, or trimurti, consisting of Brahma, Vishnu, and Shiva. Brahma is responsible for the creation of the universe; Vishnu, its preservation; and Shiva, its dissolution. Each trimurti deity is associated with one of the modalities of prakriti: *rajas*, sattva, and tamas, respectively.

To reach Īśvara, it is enough to focus upon just one of these aspects. Just as a small child can capture his or her father's attention by barely pinching one of his fingers, the human being can relate to Brahman simply by worshipping with devotion one of its aspects.

When traveling in India or visiting Hindu temples elsewhere, many people are surprised to see a variety of *mūrtis*, such as Sri Sri Rādhā-Krishna, Sītā-Rama, Lord Shiva, Gaṇeśa, or the Devi, and assume that *Sanātana-dharma* is polytheistic, as it accepts the existence of many gods. However, the truth is that all devas are mere facets of the Divine, of Īśvara.

Different lines of bhakti have emerged according to the aspect of the trimurti that inspires devotion. Although some direct their love toward Brahma, most devotees are inclined toward Vishnu or Shiva. While the principal lines are Vaishnavism and Shaivism, we cannot exclude Shaktism, which worships the Divine Mother, not as an aspect of Īśvara but as a symbol of kundalini shakti.

Just as a person has different aspects and a man can be a son to his mother, husband to his wife, father to his children, friend to his colleagues, and subordinate to his boss, Īśvara can manifest himself in a myriad aspects according to the relationship that we establish with him, without ever ceasing to be one and the same Supreme Lord. As it is stated in the *Rig Veda*:

indraṁ mitraṁ varuṇam agnim āhur
atho divyaḥ sa suparṇo garutmān
ekaṁ sad viprā bahudhā vadanty
agniṁ yamaṁ mātariśvānam āhuḥ

> They call it Indra, Mitra, Varuṇa, Agni, and the nobly winged celestial Garuḍa. The Truth is one, but the sages refer to it in various ways as Agni, Yama, Mātariśvan.
>
> (*Rig Veda*, 1.164.46)

God is one, but out of compassion, he allows himself to be contemplated in limitless aspects, revealing himself in the specific form that each bhakta is inclined to worship him. The word *iṣṭa-devatā* means "favorite or chosen deity," and refers to the preferred aspect of the Divine chosen by the devotees—or by their spiritual masters—to honor God in the personal aspect and worship him in the temple and at home. It is highly recommended to remain faithful to only one aspect of the deity throughout one's entire life. Thus, devotees are free to choose whichever aspect of the Divine appeals to their hearts. In the words of Sri Rāmakṛṣṇa Paramahaṁsa: "Many are the names of God and infinite are the forms by which one can address him. In whatever name and form one worships him, through that he will be realized."

As Patañjali notes, yogis will encounter the Divine in the aspect they conceive it:

svādhyāyād iṣṭa-devatā-saṁprayogaḥ

> Union with the preferred deity happens through study, which leads to wisdom of the Self.
>
> (*Yoga Sutra*, 2.44)

As the attitude of Hinduism is always inclusive and never exclusive, bhakti yogis do not view their *iṣṭa-devatās* as superior to others, or as the only aspect of the Divine worthy of worship. Rather, they have chosen the one aspect within which they find all the others.

Thus, when we contemplate our favorite deity, we do not perceive something different from ourselves, but our potential: what we can become. The *iṣṭa-devatā* is humanity transcending its lower nature; we are transcending ourselves.

andhaṁ tamaḥ praviśanti
ye 'sambhūtim upāsate
tato bhūya iva te tamo
ya u sambhūtyā ratāḥ

Those who worship the unmanifested enter the region of darkness, and worse still occurs to the worshippers of the manifested.

(*Īśāvāsya Upanishad*, 12)

sambhūtiṁ ca vināśaṁ ca
yas tad vedobhayaṁ saha
vināśena mṛtyuṁ tīrtvā
sambhūtyā'mṛtam aśnute

One who worships God simultaneously in his personal and impersonal aspects overcomes death through the worship of the personal and attains immortality through the worship of the impersonal.

(*Īśāvāsya Upanishad*, 14)

Consequently, our path toward the Whole must begin with the manifested because it is through the immanent God that we reach the transcendent God. We attain communion with Īśvara once we go beyond *avidya*, and we realize our identity as Absolute Brahman when we transcend maya.

Chapter 5

The nine limbs of bhakti yoga

Bhakti yoga is also called *navāṅga-yoga*, "yoga of the nine devotional limbs." They are:

- ***Śravaṇa*:** To listen to the holy pastimes (*līlās*) of the Lord.
- ***Kīrtana*:** To chant the sacred glories of the Lord.
- ***Smaraṇa*:** To constantly remember the names of the Lord and his presence in our lives.
- ***Pāda-sevana*:** To worship the sacred feet of the Lord.
- ***Arcana*:** To worship through ceremonies and rituals.
- ***Vandana*:** To prostrate, do acts of reverence and pray to the Lord.
- ***Dāsya*:** To cultivate an attitude of service toward the Lord.
- ***Sakhya*:** To cultivate friendship with the Lord.
- ***Ātma-nivedana*:** To surrender completely to the Lord.

According to the *Bhāgavata Purana* the process of bhakti marga comprises nine *aṅgas*, "limbs":

śrī-prahrāda uvāca-
śravaṇaṁ kīrtanaṁ viṣṇoḥ
smaraṇaṁ pāda-sevanam
arcanaṁ vandanaṁ dāsyaṁ
sakhyam ātma-nivedanam

iti puṁsārpitā viṣṇau
bhaktiś cen nava-lakṣaṇā
kriyeta bhagavaty addhā
tan manye 'dhītam uttamam

> Sri Prahlāda said: "I consider these nine characteristics [of devotion] to be the highest form of learning: listening to and glorifying Lord Vishnu, remembering him, serving his lotus feet, worshipping him reverently, offering him obeisance and prayers, becoming his servant, considering him one's best friend, and surrendering everything to him."
>
> (*Bhāgavata Purana*, 7.5.23-24)

Rūpa Gosvāmī describes this devotional process and makes the following comment:

sā bhaktir eka-mukhy-āṇgāśrītānaikāngikātha vā
sva-vāsanānusāreṇa niṣṭhātaḥ siddhi-kṛd bhavet

> When steadiness is attained in this bhakti, either in the primary or in the subordinate limb, according to one's natural inclination, one can achieve perfection.
>
> (*Bhakti-rasāmṛta-sindhu*, 1.2.264)

He then mentions various exemplary devotees who have attained perfection in bhakti through their complete dedication to one of the nine limbs:

śrī-viṣṇoḥ śravaṇe parīkṣid abhavad vaiyāsakiḥ kīrtane
prahlādaḥ smaraṇe tad-aṅghri-bhajane lakṣmīḥ pṛthuḥ pūjane
akrūras tv abhivandane kapi-patir dāsye 'tha sakhye 'rjunaḥ
sarvasvātma-nivedane balir abhūt kṛṣṇāptir eṣāṁ param

> Maharaja Parīkṣit attained the highest perfection simply by listening about Lord Vishnu, Śukadeva by glorifying him, Prahlāda by remembering the Lord, and Lakṣmī by worshipping the feet of Mahāviṣṇu. Maharaja Pṛthu attained similar perfection by venerating the Lord, and Akrūra, by offering him prayers. Hanuman attained perfection by being a servant of Lord Rāmacandra, Arjuna, by being Krishna's friend, and Bali Maharaja by dedicating everything to the lotus feet of Krishna.
>
> (*Bhakti-rasāmṛta-sindhu*, 1.2.265)

These *aṅgas* are also described in the *Vishnu Purana*. They are generally praised in the scriptures as gates that lead to the highest goal of the devotional process for every human being, regardless of caste, faith, or religion:

tasmāt sarvātmanā rājan
hariḥ sarvatra sarvadā
śrotavyaḥ kīrtitavyaś ca
smartavyo bhagavān nṛṇām

> O King, it is essential that every human being hears, glorifies and remembers the Lord with their whole being, always and everywhere.
> (*Bhāgavata Purana*, 2.2.36)

śravaṇa-kīrtana ha-ite kṛṣṇe haya 'premā'
sei pañcama puruṣārtha-puruṣārthera sīmā

> Upon reaching the level of divine love toward Lord Krishna by listening, glorifying [and the other limbs], one attains the fifth stage of perfection [beyond dharma, artha, kama, and even moksha] and the pinnacle of life's goals.
> (*Caitanya-caritāmṛta*, "*Madhya-līlā*," 9.261)

These nine limbs do not separate stages or distinct levels; they are interrelated. We will now discuss each of them in depth.

Śravaṇa, "listening"

Śravaṇa means "listening" and refers specifically to the act of listening to stories about the *līlās*, "pastimes," of the Lord spoken by one's spiritual master or other saintly souls and sages. The *gopīs* describe *śravaṇa* in this way:

tava kathāmṛtaṁ tapta-jīvanaṁ
kavibhir īḍitaṁ kalmaṣāpaham
śravaṇa-maṅgalaṁ śrīmad ātataṁ
bhuvi gṛṇanti te bhūri-dā janāḥ

> O Krishna, your nectarous pastimes narrated by enlightened souls revive the afflicted and distressed. They eliminate all impurities and to hear them is auspicious and glorious. Benevolent are those who praise you and spread this nectar upon the earth.
>
> (*Bhāgavata Purana*, 10.31.9)

Although disciples can read these narrations for themselves, it is recommended to hear them from the lips of one's guru, as noted by Śrīla Viśvanātha Cakravartī Ṭhākur:

ānuśravaṁ guror uccāraṇam anuśrūyante

> [Devotees] should learn about the Lord by listening to their spiritual master.
>
> (*Śrimad-bhāgavatam śārārtha-darśinī,* 11.6.19)

Śravaṇa has the capacity to awaken an aspiration for the divinity within us, as affirmed in this verse:

nivṛtta-tarṣair upagīyamānād
bhavauṣadhāc chrotra-mano-'bhirāmāt
ka uttama-śloka-guṇānuvādāt
pumān virajyeta vinā paśughnāt

Those who remain aloof from material desires and are liberated from them, delight in hearing the qualities of the Lord described and glorified. Listening to these glories is the remedy for worldly existence and gives happiness to the ears and the mind. Therefore, who would not delight in listening to them besides a butcher [of his own soul]?

(*Bhāgavata Purana*, 10.1.4)

idaṁ hi puṁsas tapasaḥ śrutasya vā
sviṣṭasya sūktasya ca buddhi-dattayoḥ
avicyuto 'rthaḥ kavibhir nirūpito
yad-uttama-śloka-guṇānuvarṇanam

The enlightened sages have declared that the eternal purpose of one's austerity is recounting the virtues of the Lord, who is of excellent fame, and study of the Vedas, sacrifices, the singing of hymns, enlightenment, and charity.

(*Bhāgavata Purana*, 1.5.22)

In this first step on the path of devotion, we become accessible and open to receive the seed of devotion from a spiritual master in the fertile soil of our heart. Jīva Gosvāmī states:

> *tataś ca viśeṣa-bubhutsāyāṁ satyānteṣv ekato 'nekato vā śrī-gurutvenāśritāc chravaṇaṁ kriyate.*

> [When] one desires to advance spiritually, one should take the shelter of an initiating guru (*dīkṣa*) or several instructing gurus (*śikṣā*), and listen (*śravana*). In this way, the Truth will be understood from beginning to end.
>
> (*Bhakti-sandarbha*, 202.11)

Devotion cannot be learned intellectually, as it is not a matter of methods or techniques. *Prema*, "sacred and pure love," is like a virus that can only be caught through contact with someone who carries it. Thus, we might say that pure devotees of the Lord are those who have been transformed into tremendously contagious elements of devotion.

Herein lies the great importance of *sādhu-saṅga*, "the company of great souls," and satsang, "association with a sage who has realized the Truth." While *śravaṇa* mainly refers to the narration of the pastimes of the Lord, the *Bhāgavata Purana* also recommends listening to descriptions of the qualities of saints:

> *śrutasya puṁsāṁ sucira-śramasya*
> *nanv añjasā sūribhir īḍito 'rthaḥ*

yat-tad-guṇānuśravaṇaṁ mukunda-
pādāravindaṁ hṛdayeṣu yeṣām

> The conclusion of the wise is that the highest goal of *śruta*, "knowledge received by hearing," attained only after great and prolonged effort, is listening to the manifold praises of the qualities of those who carry the lotus feet of Lord Mukunda in their hearts.
>
> (*Bhāgavata Purana*, 3.13.4)

To listen with precision requires silence, as we cannot simultaneously speak and grasp what another person is conveying. As silence intensifies, attention sharpens. In this way, *śravaṇa* requires disciples to create internal stillness. This does not consist in a mere lack of noise and sound, but in the absence of preconceived ideas, concepts, conclusions, and fluctuations of the mind. Certainly, the first step on the ladder of bhakti is the cultivation of receptivity.

Just as the food we eat becomes part of our organism, when disciples listen carefully to their master, teachings are absorbed, providing the necessary vitamins to grow and evolve. Disciples may forget the exact words, but the wisdom of the master becomes part of their souls.

Cultivate listening. When you have health-related questions, listen to your body; when you hesitate about the direction of your life, listen cautiously to existence itself in the depths of your heart. One who cultivates and develops the art of listening with vigilant receptivity finds silence and peace.

Kīrtana, "glorification"

In Sanskrit, the word *kīrtana* means "to glorify the Lord by harmoniously chanting his holy names." Glorification elevates energy, intensifies devotion, and is certainly one of the most rapid and accessible paths to experiencing God. *Kīrtana* is congregational singing, in which a *kīrtanakar* sings the mantra and a group of people responds. The singing is accompanied by musical instruments like the tabla, mridanga, harmonium, hand cymbals called *kartālas*, and other instruments. *Kīrtana* is much more than mere entertainment or amusement. Rather, it is transformational singing.

The practice of *kīrtana-yoga* is recommended for everyone in this fallen age of Kali.

dhyāyan kṛte yajan yajñais
tretāyāṁ dvāpare 'rcayan
yad āpnoti tad āpnoti
kalau saṅkīrtya keśavam

> What is experienced in Satya Yuga through meditation, in Treta Yuga through sacrifices, and in Dvapara Yuga through worship can be experienced in Kali Yuga by chanting (*kīrtana*) the name of Lord Keśava.
>
> (*Vishnu Purana*, 6.2.17)

Nowadays, very few are willing to accept the austerity required for classic yoga paths. Hatha yoga, raja yoga, and jnana yoga are suitable for an exclusive minority because they demand strict discipline. On the contrary, *kīrtana-yoga* is available to everyone and can benefit the masses.

Many saints, yogis, and mystics have composed a myriad of beautiful bhajanas, "devotional songs," that glorify the Lord while they were in a state of divine consciousness. With brilliant clarity, the Bhagavad Gita indicates that *kīrtana* is the principal occupation of great souls:

satataṁ kīrtayanto māṁ
yatantaś ca dṛḍha-vratāḥ
namasyantaś ca māṁ bhaktyā
nitya-yuktā upāsate

> Always glorifying me with great effort and determination and prostrating before me, [these great souls are] ever steadfast in their devoted worship of me.
>
> (Bhagavad Gita, 9.14)

Devotees glorify their own *iṣṭa-devatā*. Thus, devotees of Lord Krishna chant the *mahā-mantra*: "*Hare kṛṣṇa hare kṛṣṇa, kṛṣṇa kṛṣṇa hare hare, hare rāma hare rāma, rāma rāma hare hare*"; devotees of Lord Shiva intone mantras like: "*Oṁ namaḥ śivāya*"; Shaktas, devotees of the Divine Mother, chant the mantra: "*Oṁ śrī mahā-kālikāyai namo namaḥ*," among others.

Śukadeva says the following words to Maharaja Parīkṣit:

etan-nirvidyamānānām
icchatām akuto-bhayam
yogināṁ nṛpa nirṇītaṁ
harer nāmānukīrtanam

O King, it is affirmed that the constant chanting of the holy names of the Lord [is the way] for yogis who have developed aversion to this world and seek to attain the fearless state.

(*Bhāgavata Purana*, 2.1.11)

Saṅkīrtana refers to a more elaborate or complete glorification. The Sanskrit prefix *saṅ* indicates "fullness" or "to be accompanied by." *Saṅkīrtana* is "congregational singing" or "chanting accompanied by musical instruments"; it is performed in the temple as well as in the home with family and friends. Its style varies according to the tradition of each region.

Sri Chaitanya (1486-1533 CE) was a great Vaishnava saint who began a very important *saṅkīrtana* movement of the *mahā-mantra* in Bengal.

The *mahā-mantra* is especially recommended for *saṅkīrtana* in this current age. This is confirmed by the Upanishad of the *Krishna Yajur Veda*, where Brahma answers Sage Nārada's question:

hariḥ oṁ. dvāparānte nārado brahmāṇam jagaṁ katham bhagavan gāṁ paryaṭan-kaliṁ santareyam iti. sa hovāca brahmā sādhu pṛṣṭo 'smi sarva śṛti-rahasyaṁ gopyaṁ tac chṛṇu yena kali-saṁsāraṁ tariṣyasi. bhāgavata ādi-puruṣasya nārāyaṇasya nāmoccāraṇa-mātreṇa nirdhṛta-kalir bhavatīti.

Hari Oṁ! At the end of Dvapara Yuga, Nārada, who had traversed the whole world, went to Brahma and addressed him thus: "O Lord, how shall I be able to ward off the effects of Kali Yuga?" Brahma replied, "You have asked an excellent question. Listen to the secret that all Vedas keep hidden, by which one may go beyond material existence during the age of Kali. One becomes free from the influence of Kali Yuga by merely uttering the names of Lord Nārāyaṇa.

(*Kali-santaraṇa Upanishad*, verse 1)

nāradaḥ punaḥ papraccha taraṇaṁ kim iti sa hovaca hiraṇyagarbaḥ—

hare rāma hare rāma
rāma rāma hare hare
hare kṛṣṇa hare kṛṣṇa
kṛṣṇa kṛṣṇa hare hare

iti ṣoḍaśakaṁ nāmnāṁ
kali-kalmaśa-nāśanam
nātaḥ para-taropāyaḥ
sarva-vedeṣu dṛśyate

> Nārada asked Brahma again, "What are those names?" Lord Brahma replied, "*Hare Rāma Hare Rāma Rāma Rāma Hare Hare, Hare Kṛṣṇa Hare Kṛṣṇa Kṛṣṇa Kṛṣṇa Hare Hare.*" These sixteen holy names will destroy the sinful influences of the age of Kali. I do not see any other method.
>
> (*Kali-santaraṇa Upanishad*, verse 2)

The infinite shakti that lies in the holy names of the Lord is able to remove all *mala*, "mental impurity." *Saṅkīrtana* helps overcome obstacles on the path to self-realization.

It is preferable to chant *kīrtana* in the original Sanskrit. It can be chanted in two different moods: *sambhoga-bhāva* and *vipralambha-bhāva*. *Sambhoga-bhāva* means to chant with a "mood of enjoyment" out of happiness for being in direct association with the Lord; *vipralambha-bhāva* means to chant in a "mood of separation" out of longing due to being separated from him.

The two main types of *kīrtana* are: *nāma-kīrtana* and *līlā-kīrtana*.

1. *Nāma-kīrtana*: chanting the divine names of our *iṣṭa-devatā*. By singing with devotion, devotees associate directly with the Lord, because on the absolute plane, God and his name are one and the same. In India, events called *akhaṇḍa-nāma-kīrtana* are held. *Akhaṇḍa* means "continuous" and these *kīrtanas* can take place nonstop for up to a week, led by musical groups who usually replace each other every hour or two

2. *Līlā-kīrtana*: another type of devotional chanting that describes the various pastimes of the Lord. Among the most popular types of *līlā-kīrtana* we have:
   i. *Pāla-kīrtana*: singing certain pastimes of one's *iṣṭa-devatā*, accompanied by a group of devotees.
   ii. *Padyāvalī-kīrtana*: singing the divine pastimes of Krishna and his various associates.
   iii. *Aṣṭa-kālīya-kīrtana*: singing a full day's pastimes of the divine couple, Their Lordships Sri Sri Rādhā and Krishna for twenty-four hours starting at 6 am.
   iv. *Dhun*: although it is not performed with mantras, both the names of the Lord and his pastimes are glorified. Its devotional benefit is similar to *kīrtana*. It is popular in the area of Gujarat, India, and is usually performed in *sambhoga-bhāva*.

Since it originates in sound, *kīrtana* shares origins with the sacred Vedas. It purifies the atmosphere, opens our hearts to divine grace, transforms our feelings into devotion, and channels them toward the Absolute.

Any yogic process would be incomplete without *kīrtana*. It leads us to states in which the senses are turned deeply inward, allowing us to transcend the mental plane. *Kīrtana* is certainly the simplest and most effective means of spiritual elevation; it is the divine nectar that can quench the spiritual thirst of souls lost in the worldly desert of illusion.

Chant the holy names of the Lord with devotion from the depths of your heart. Put yourself in God until you melt in his presence.

Smaraṇa, "remembrance"

Smaraṇa means "remembrance"; it is the constant remembering of God. *Smaraṇa* is actually an organic consequence of the two previous steps, *śravaṇa* and *kīrtana*. Remembrance of God happens spontaneously after listening to his glories and pastimes and singing his holy names. *Smaraṇa* is not a practice, but an effect of the previous processes; it is not the product of any effort, but rather it blossoms naturally.

When we try to remember the name of a childhood friend, we get stressed and mentally blocked; but in a moment of relaxation, the name emerges from our memory on its own. Similarly, *smaraṇa* is an awakening that happens in a moment of mental tranquility and emotional peace.

In Upanishadic literature, the term *smaraṇa* implies "observation," just as *sammasat* implies "correct attention" for Buddha. In the terminology of Caitanya, we say that *smaraṇa* is like cleaning the mirror of the heart from the accumulated dust that obscures divine glory.

In the *Vishnu Purana*, we find beautiful verses in which Prahlāda, the great devotee of the Lord, declares:

prayāsaḥ smaraṇe ko 'sya
smṛto yacchati śobhanam
pāpa-kṣayaś ca bhavati
smaratāṁ tam ahar-niśam

sarva-bhūta-sthite tasmin
matir maitrī divā-niśam

bhavatāṁ jāyatām evaṁ
sarva-kleśān prahāsyatha

> What difficulty is there in remembering the one who, when remembered day and night, bestows all that is auspicious and removes all sins? Let all your thoughts and affections be fixed upon the one present in all beings, and you shall let go of all anguish.
>
> (*Vishnu Purana*, 1.17.78–79)

In the *Mukunda-mālā Stotra* by Kulaśekhara Ālvār, we read:

kṛṣṇa tvadīya-pada-paṅkaja-pañjarāntam
adyaiva me viśatu mānasa-rāja-haṁsaḥ
prāṇa-prayāṇa-samaye kapha-vāta-pittaiḥ
kaṇṭhāvarodhana-vidhau smaraṇaṁ kutas te

> O Lord Krishna! Be so kind as to allow my mind's royal swan to enter the tangled stalks of your lotus feet. How will I be able to remember you at the moment of death when my throat is choked up with mucus, bile, and air?
>
> (*Mukunda-mālā Stotra*, 33)

The remembrance of God, our *iṣṭa-devatā*, and the sacred stories related to him should be ceaseless. Just as alcoholics are unable to forget drinks, smokers cigarettes, or penny-pinchers money, devotees are so firmly attached to their *iṣṭa-devatās* that they remember the Lord, his name, his saintly devotees, or the spiritual master, day and night, even when dreaming.

etāvān sāṅkhya-yogābhyāṁ
sva-dharma-pariniṣṭhayā
janma-lābhaḥ paraḥ puṁsām
ante nārāyaṇa-smṛtiḥ

> The highest perfection of human life is to be able to remember God at the moment of death; it is attained through self-knowledge, yoga, and a life in accordance with dharma.
>
> (*Bhāgavata Purana*, 2.1.6)

Forgetting our true essence causes unhappiness and suffering. There is no evil in humans, only ignorance of our true divine origin. Remembrance of God is forgetfulness of illusion, or maya, duality, and the relative world. The spiritual process consists of forgetting the theoretical plane, to stop living in a world of hypothesis and ideas, and to begin moving in the realm of real facts.

Constant remembrance of God leads us to forget what we imagine we are and thoughts about ourselves—our ideas, concepts, beliefs, opinions, and conclusions—and brings back the memory of who we really are. The remembrance of God is to forget our identity, in order to remember what we never knew. It is simply self-remembrance, reminding us of ourselves.

Smaraṇa does not mean remembering what *was*, but what *is*; it consists of the oblivion of the past and the remembrance of the present. It is not related to thought, but to the heart, which holds the divine memory of our true nature.

Smaraṇa suggests that we have not lost God, but we have forgotten him; it does not suggest transforming ourselves into what we have never been, but simply being the only thing that we can be. *Smaraṇa* is the essence of enlightenment. It is not striving to find something that we do not possess: God is here, he is life itself. It is impossible to lose him or abandon him, we can only forget him.

Playing roles to be loved and accepted, we have forgotten who we really are. Religion merely suggests that if we live like beggars, it is because we have forgotten that we are sons of the king; if we fear death, it is because we have forgotten our eternal nature; if we suffer, it is only because we have forgotten that we are joy itself. So it is not about remembering, but being. We are the forgotten divine.

Pāda-sevana, "service to the feet"

In Sanskrit, *pāda* means "foot," and *sevana* means "service or attendance." We dedicate much of our time to helping others: we serve our employers, our families, society, and so on. Service means responding to the demands and needs of others, but what type of service can we offer the omnipotent God, who needs no assistance? It is not God, but devotees who need to express devotion in practice through service.

Following *śravaṇa* (hearing about the Lord), *kīrtana* (glorifying him), and *smaraṇa* (remembering him), devotees naturally seek the intimacy of devotional service. *Pāda-sevana* is mentioned after *smaraṇa* because it should be an expression of the joy of remembering the Divine. Philanthropy motivated by personal gain is not real devotional service. If we help others in order to reach heaven ourselves, then we are merely using others to fulfill our ambitions.

An old Hindu story describes an extremely ambitious man. After reaching the conclusion that service in this life is inevitable, he wanted to serve the most important and powerful person. He went to his village and became the head servant of the mayor. One day, a tax collector visited the village and took money from the mayor. The ambitious man left the village with the tax collector to become his assistant and helped him collect money from other mayors. Upon arriving at the capital, the tax collector brought all the funds to the governor. The man saw that the tax collector was subordinate to the governor so he asked to be the governor's secretary. The governor brought the new secretary to visit the king. In the royal court, the ambitious servant realized it was the king whom he should be serving. He became one of the king's servants. One day, he noticed that the king entered the temple and bowed down, venerating Lord Krishna. Finally, the man understood who is really worthy of being served and became a devotee of the Lord.

There are those who believe that devoting themselves entirely to the service of the Lord is irresponsible, because we have many other obligations in life. On that, this verse says:

devarṣi-bhūtāpta-nṛṇāṁ pitṛṇāṁ
na kiṅkaro nāyam ṛṇī ca rājan
sarvātmanā yaḥ śaraṇaṁ śaraṇyaṁ
gato mukundaṁ parihṛtya kartam

> Anyone who has taken shelter at the lotus feet of Mukunda (Krishna) the liberator, has given up all obligations, and has taken the path in all seriousness, has neither duties nor obligations to demigods, sages, living entities, family members, humankind, or ancestors.
>
> (*Bhāgavata Purana*, 11.5.41)

In the same scripture, we read the following verses:

yat-pāda-sevābhirucis tapasvinām
aśeṣa-janmopacitam malaṁ dhiyaḥ

sadyaḥ kṣiṇoty anvaham edhatī satī
yathā padāṅguṣṭha-viniḥsṛtā sarit

Like the water [of the Ganges] that emanates from God's toes, taking pleasure in the service to his lotus feet instantly cleanses the impurity accumulated in [the mind of] miserable human beings over countless births, and [their purity] increases daily.

(*Bhāgavata Purana*, 4.21.31)

sa veda dhātuḥ padavīṁ parasya
duranta-vīryasya rathāṅga-pāṇeḥ
yo 'māyayā santatayānuvṛttyā
bhajeta tat-pāda-saroja-gandham

Only one who offers whole-hearted, continuous, and beneficial service unto the fragrant lotus feet of the Lord, who holds the discus in his hand [Krishna], can know the creator of the universe in his full glory, power, and transcendence.

(*Bhāgavata Purana*, 1.3.38)

tais tāny aghāni pūyante
tapo-dāna-vratādibhiḥ
nādharmajaṁ tad-dhṛdayaṁ
tad apīśāṅghri-sevayā

Although one may atone for the actions of a sinful life through austerity, acts of charity, vows, and

> other methods, it is not possible to uproot material desires from one's heart with these pious activities. However, by serving the lotus feet of the Lord, one is immediately freed of all such impurities.
> (*Bhāgavata Purana*, 6.2.17)

By performing devotional service, devotees become so content that their sole desire is to serve at the lotus feet of the Lord.

dhautātmā puruṣaḥ kṛṣṇa-
pāda-mūlaṁ na muñcati
mukta-sarva-parikleśaḥ
pānthaḥ sva-śaraṇaṁ yathā

> Once the heart has been purified [through the process of devotional service], pure devotees can never abandon the lotus feet of the Lord which completely satisfies them, just as travelers feel content and free of all troubles upon reaching home after a difficult voyage.
> (*Bhāgavata Purana*, 2.8.6)

We believe we are the owners of our senses and use them for our own gratification. However, bhakti yogis who see that the body is born, develops, ages, and eventually dies understand that it does not belong to them; it is only a loan. Therefore, devotees are able to recognize God as the authentic Lord of the senses, and consequently, place their bodies in complete service and at the disposal of their master. Through devotional service, bhaktas become conscious of the fact that all the things they thought to be theirs, including their own lives, are nothing but possessions of God. On this topic, there is the example of Maharaja Ambarīṣa, who is mentioned in the *Bhāgavata Purana*:

sa vai manaḥ kṛṣṇa-padāravindayor
vacāṁsi vaikuṇṭha-guṇānuvarṇane
karau harer mandira-mārjanādiṣu
śrutiṁ cakārācyuta-sat-kathodaye
mukunda-liṅgālaya-darśane dṛśau
tad-bhṛtya-gātra-sparśe 'ṅga-saṅgamam
ghrāṇaṁ ca tat-pāda-saroja-saurabhe
śrīmat-tulasyā rasanāṁ tad-arpite
pādau hareḥ kṣetra-padānusarpaṇe
śiro hṛṣīkeśa-padābhivandane
kāmaṁ ca dāsye na tu kāma-kāmyayā
yathottama-śloka-janāśrayā ratiḥ

Maharaja Ambarīṣa set his mind to constantly meditate on the lotus feet of Krishna, his words to praise the glories of the Lord, his hands to cleanse the Lord's temple and holy places, and his ears to hear words spoken by or about Krishna. He used his eyes to see the deity, Krishna's temples, and places where Krishna had lived, such as Mathura and Vrindavana. He used his sense of touch to touch the feet of the Lord's devotees, his olfactory senses to smell the fragrance of holy Tulasi offered to the Lord, his tongue to taste the Lord's *prasāda*. Maharaja Ambarīṣa used his legs to walk to the holy places and temples of the Lord, his head to bow at the feet of the Lord, and his senses and all his desires to serve the Lord. Maharaja Ambarīṣa used each and every enjoyable thing only for God's service, but not out of any personal interest. His passionate love for the Lord was like the love of those great devotees who take complete shelter in the Lord.

(*Bhāgavata Purana*, 9.4.18–20)

Sanātana Gosvāmī, the illustrious disciple of Sri Chaitanya, listed in his book *Hari-bhakti-vilāsa* the five principles of devotional service followed by *Gauḍīya* Vaishnava devotees.

1. Worship the deity.
2. Listen to the *Bhāgavata Purana*.
3. Associate with devotees.
4. Practice *saṅkīrtana*.
5. Live in the holy city of Mathura.

He also listed sixty-four principles with ten being primary principles meant for beginners:

1. Accept the shelter of a qualified spiritual master's lotus feet.
2. Be initiated by a spiritual master and learn how to accept devotional service from him or her.

3. Abide by the spiritual master's orders with faith and devotion.
4. Follow the paths of great acharyas (teachers) under the spiritual master's guidance.
5. Ask the spiritual master how to progress in expanding your divine consciousness.
6. While engaged in devotional service, be ready to give up things that you like and accept things that you may not desire, solely for the satisfaction of the Divine.
7. Live in a sacred place of pilgrimage, such as Dvārakā or Vrindavana.
8. Accept only what is essential and deal with the material world only as much as is necessary.
9. Fast on Ekādaśī, the eleventh day of every fortnight.
10. Worship sacred trees, such as the banyan.

The ten secondary regulative principles help devotees achieve the level of practical devotional service, or sadhana bhakti.

1. Firmly avoid the association of non-devotees.
2. Do not instruct one who does not desire devotional service.
3. Stand against the construction of costly temples or monasteries.
4. Do not endeavor to read too many books or live off lectures or readings of the *Bhāgavata Purana* or Bhagavad Gita.
5. Do not neglect ordinary dealings.

6. Keep yourself from falling into bouts of sorrow in times of loss or bouts of joy in times of plenty.
7. Respect every manifestation of God.
8. Refrain from causing unnecessary problems for any living creature.
9. Avoid making offenses while chanting the sacred name of the Lord or when worshipping the deity in the temple.
10. Do not tolerate blasphemy of the Divine or his devotees.

Forty-four additional activities of devotional service:

1. Decorate the body with tilak, the sign of the Vaishnavas, to remind others of Krishna.
2. When applying tilak, one may sometimes write "*Hare Kṛṣṇa*" on the body.
3. Accept flowers and garlands that have been offered to the deity and the guru by putting them on your body.
4. Learn to dance in front of the deity.
5. Bow down immediately upon seeing the deity or spiritual master.
6. Stand up upon seeing a temple of Lord Krishna.
7. When a devotee realizes that the deity is being taken in a street procession, join the procession immediately.
8. Visit a Vishnu temple once or twice daily, in the morning and the evening.
9. One must circumambulate the outside of the temple at least three times.

10. Follow the guiding principles when worshipping the deity in the temple by offering light and food, decorating the deity, and so forth.
11. Perform personal service to the deities.
12. Sing to the Lord.
13. Perform *saṅkīrtana*.
14. Chant the Lord's holy names.
15. Pray.
16. Recite well-known prayers.
17. Eat a small portion of food from the plate offered to the deities.
18. Drink *caraṇāmṛta*, "the water that bathed the feet of the deities."
19. Smell the incense and flowers offered to the deity.
20. Touch the deity's lotus feet.
21. Gaze at the deity with deep devotion.
22. Offer light (*ārati*) at different times.
23. Listen to the Lord's pastimes from the *Bhāgavata Purana*, Bhagavad Gita, and other devotional books.
24. Pray to the deity for mercy.
25. Remember the deity.
26. Meditate on the deity.
27. Offer volunteer service.
28. Think of the Lord as your friend.
29. Offer all that you have to the Lord.
30. Offer a favorite item, such as food or clothing.
31. Take risks of all sorts and perform all endeavors for the benefit of Krishna.
32. In all circumstances, be a surrendered soul.
33. Water the Tulasi tree.

34. Listen to readings of the *Bhāgavata Purana* and similar literature regularly.
35. Reside in a sacred place such as Mathura, Vrindavana, or Dvārakā.
36. Offer service to other Vaishnava devotees.
37. Plan your devotional service according to your resources.
38. Arrange special services in the month of Kārttika (October/November).
39. Observe a special ceremony on Krishna's appearance day, Janmāṣṭamī.
40. All that is done for the deity should be conducted with great care and devotion.
41. Revel in the pleasure of the *Bhāgavata Purana* by reading it with devotees rather than outsiders.
42. Associate with more advanced devotees.
43. Chant the holy name of the Lord.
44. Live in the region of Mathura.

For the bhakti yogi, love for God is not theoretical but tangible and is expressed through actions and assistance given to others. *Pāda-sevana* is bhakti flowing through karma yoga; it is the love of God that reaches everyone through this service. Since service represents the active aspect of love, great acharyas consider *pāda-sevana* a synonym for bhakti. In this way, they have defined bhakti yoga as devotional service, because offering aid to humanity is the practical manifestation of love.

In Śrīla Rūpa Gosvāmī's *Bhakti-rasāmṛta-sindhu* (1.1.12), we find an example of this, quoting a verse from the renowned *Nārada-pañca-rātra*. It is also mentioned by Kṛṣṇadāsa Kavirāja Gosvāmī:

sarvopādhi-vinirmuktaṁ
tat-paratvena nirmalam
hṛṣīkeṇa hṛṣīkeśa-
sevanaṁ bhaktir ucyate

Bhakti is service to the Lord by using the senses in the service of the master of the senses. This must be done by renouncing personal ambitions and without any desire except the intention to please the Lord.
(*Śrī-caitanya-caritāmṛta*, "*Madhya-līlā*," 19.170)

Pāda-sevana finds its maximum expression in Lakṣmī, the goddess of fortune, who massages the feet of Lord Vishnu.

śrīr yat padāmbuja-rajaś cakame tulasyā
labdhvā 'pi vakṣasi padaṁ kila bhṛtya-juṣṭam
yasyāḥ sva-vīkṣaṇa utānya-sura-prayāsas
tadvad vayaṁ ca tava pāda-rajaḥ prapannāḥ

Goddess Lakṣmī, whose glance is sought with great effort by the other gods, has achieved the unique position of always remaining on the chest of her Lord, Nārāyaṇa. Still, along with Tulasī Devi and the Lord's many other servants, she too desires the dust of his lotus feet. Similarly, we approach the dust of your lotus feet for shelter.
(*Bhāgavata Purana*, 10.29.37)

Pāda-sevana is to humbly approach the feet of the Lord, as even the goddess of fortune does. Devotees do not beg the Lord for wealth because they understand that fortune does not serve them but the Lord. Power and riches are destined for the service of the Lord since they are the materialization of Lakṣmī Devi, the loving devotee of the Lord.

yady apy asau pārśva-gato raho-gatas
tathāpi tasyāghri-yugaṁ navaṁ navam
pade pade kā virameta tat-padāc
calāpi yac chrīr na jahāti karhicit

Although Lord Sri Krishna was constantly by their side, as well as exclusively alone, his feet seemed to them to be newer and newer. The goddess of fortune, although by nature always restless and moving, could not walk away from the Lord's feet. Therefore, what woman could detach herself from those feet, having once taken shelter in them?

(*Bhāgavata Purana*, 1.11.33)

Most human beings have experienced the restless nature of Lakṣmī, the goddess of fortune. No one has managed to control her even though many have spent their lives trying. People wonder why Lakṣmī does not show her generosity toward devotees who pray to the Lord for material benefits. The answer is that sincere devotees never use moments of intimate association with the Lord for material benefit.

Authentic devotion can manifest itself when our requests are denied and our prayers for material goods go unanswered. True devotion is expressed when, despite our poverty and calamities, we continue to take shelter at God's feet.

Even today, Indian tradition says that children must touch the feet of their parents and elders as a sign of respect. Touching someone's feet is a sign of deep humility. While touching the feet of an ordinary person is not always pleasant, the mere thought of the lotus feet of the Lord inspires and fills the hearts of devotees with love. The inhabitants of Vrindavana were filled with ecstasy upon seeing the footprints left by the Lord's feet, which are described in great detail in the scriptures.

samāśritā ye pada-pallava-plavaṁ
mahat-padaṁ puṇya-yaśo murāreḥ
bhavāmbudhir vatsa-padaṁ paraṁ padaṁ
padaṁ padaṁ yad vipadāṁ na teṣām

> For those who have accepted the boat of the lotus feet of the Lord, who is the shelter of the cosmic manifestation and is as famous as Murāri (the enemy of the demon Mura), the ocean of the material world is like water in a calf's hoof print. Their goal is *paraṁ padam*, or Vaikuṇṭha, the place where there are no material miseries, not the place where there is danger at every step.
> (*Bhāgavata Purana*, 10.14.58)

To serve others is equivalent to serving God, because we are a divine manifestation, as affirmed in this verse:

mamaivāṁśo jīva-loke
jīva-bhūtaḥ sanātanaḥ
manaḥ-ṣaṣṭhānīndriyāṇi
prakṛti-sthāni karṣati

> An eternal part of myself, having returned to be an individual in the world of living beings, is attracted to the five senses that, along with the sixth, the mind, abide in nature.
>
> (Bhagavad Gita, 15.7)

This was similarly expressed by Sri Rāmakṛṣṇa Paramahaṁsa: "God is everywhere, but he reaches his highest expression in man. Therefore, serve man as God, since it is as beneficial as worshipping God."

Our efforts to help the needy must arise as an offering of devotion to the Lord, as mentioned by Lord Krishna:

yat karoṣi yad aśnāsi
yaj juhoṣi dadāsi yat
yat tapasyasi kaunteya
tat kuruṣva mad-arpaṇam

> All that you do, all that you eat, all that you offer or give, as well as the austerities that you perform, O son of Kuntī, do them as an offering to me.
>
> (Bhagavad Gita, 9.27)

However, if we wish to serve humanity, we first need to know what will truly benefit others. Throughout history, dictators and tyrants have murdered millions of people believing they were providing a great service to humanity. Terrorists have attacked and killed innocent people, convinced that the sacrifice of lives served their cause. Similarly, we may give poor people sweets, believing it to be charitable, but if they are diabetic, we will actually harm them. Therefore, just as our assistance to a patient should be offered only according to a doctor's instructions, our devotional service should be carried out solely under the guidance of a spiritual master and in accordance with the holy scriptures.

The sacred feet of God are actually all of humanity, without distinctions of social class, race, gender, or religion. Therefore, *pāda-sevana* consists in striving for the benefit of all and making sacrifices for their well-being. We must cease to live selfishly, concerned only with what we can receive from others. Instead, let us cultivate *pāda-sevana* and contribute, even in a small way, to the happiness of others.

Arcana, "worship"

Arcana refers to the worship of God. It is reverence and devotion of the *upāsaka*, "devoted worshipper," directed at a deity in various ceremonies. Rūpa Gosvāmī defines *arcana*:

śuddhi-nyāsādi-purvāṅga-
karma-nirvāha-pūrvakam
arcanaṁ tūpacārāṇāṁ
syān mantreṇopapādanam

> *Arcana* is defined as the offering of articles of worship (*upacāras*) accompanied by mantras, after having performed preliminary purification activities (*pūrvāṅga-karmas*) such as *bhūta-śuddhi* and *nyāsas*.
> (*Bhakti-rasāmṛta-sindhu*, 1.2.137)

Due to its purifying effect, *arcana* allows human beings to live in peace and harmony with nature, other people, and themselves, as described in this verse:

bhrātṛvyam enaṁ tad adabhra-vīryaṁ
upekṣayādhyedhitam apramattaḥ
guror hareś caraṇopāsanāstro
jahi vyalīkaṁ svayam ātma-moṣam

> This uncontrolled mind is the greatest enemy of the living entity. If one ignores it or gives it a chance, it will grow more and more powerful and will become victorious. Although it is not factual,

it is very strong. It hides the constitutional position of the soul. O King, please try to conquer this mind with the weapon of worshipping the lotus feet of the spiritual master and of divinity. Do this with great care.

(*Bhāgavata Purana*, 5.11.17)

yāvad avabhāsayati sura-girim anuparikrāman bhagavān
ādityo vasudhā-talam ardhenaiva
pratapaty ardhenāvacchādayati tadā hi bhagavad-
upāsanopacitāti-puruṣa-prabhāvas tad anabhinandan
samajavena rathena jyotirmayena rajanīm api dinaṁ
kariṣyāmīti sapta-kṛtvas taraṇim anuparyakrāmad
dvitīya iva pataṅgaḥ

While so excellently ruling the universe, King Priyavrata once became dissatisfied with the circumambulation of the most powerful sun-god. Encircling Sumeru Hill on his chariot, the sun-god illuminated all the surrounding planetary systems. However, when the sun was on the northern side of the hill, the south received less light, and when the sun was in the south, the north received less. King Priyavrata disliked this situation and therefore decided to create daylight in the part of the universe where it was night. He followed the orbit of the sun-god on a brilliant chariot and thus fulfilled his desire. He could perform such wonderful deeds because of the power he had achieved by worshipping divinity.

(*Bhāgavata Purana*, 5.1.30)

Every religion has its own ceremonies, pilgrimages, festivals, and rituals for different events in life (birth, marriage, etc.). The wise Vedic devotees have bequeathed us vibrant rituals for the benefit of humanity. Thousands of years before the rituals of any other religion were performed, these *Sanātana-dharma* ceremonies were being taught and practiced in India. Hindus residing in Western countries make great efforts to preserve their religion. Unfortunately, the next Hindu generation is becoming distanced from its religious and spiritual roots in today's exaggerated materialism and is unaware of the great wisdom contained in these ancient ceremonies and their esoteric features. It is our duty to try to keep the flame of this magnificent wisdom alight.

Puja and *arcana*

Puja is the ceremony in which God is worshipped in the *Sanātana-dharma* religion. The word *pūjā* is derived from the Sanskrit root *pūj*, meaning "to worship, honor, or revere." It can be a ritual of gratitude as well as a glorification of the *mūrti*, "an image that represents an aspect of God," the spiritual master, great personages, or important visitors.

Both puja and *arcana* involve the worship a deity, but the former is a more formal ceremony and the latter is performed primarily by pilgrims during temple visits. Puja is the daily ceremony that includes sixteen offerings that will be described later in this chapter. *Arcana*, on the other hand, is a ceremony performed by a *pūjāka*, "priest," at the request of devotees who visit the temple bearing items to be ritually offered to the deity. At the end of the *arcana*, these offerings are returned to the visitors as the blessing of God, or *prasāda*.

Puja is described in the scriptures in two ways: the worship of the deity's image (*mūrti-pūjā*), recommended in Tantric texts, and the worship of the divinity's abstract form (*nirguṇa-pūjā*), frequently mentioned in the Vedic literature. Although the Vedas mainly describe worship and offerings to the abstract deity, we can also identify indirect references to the worship of physical manifestations of the deity.

catvāri śṛṅgā trayo asya pādā dve śīrṣe
sapta hastā so asya

He has four horns, three feet, two heads and seven hands.

(*Rig Veda*, 4.58.3)

ehy aśmānam ātiṣṭhāśmā bhavatu te tanūḥ

[O Lord,] please come dwell in this [*mūrti* made of] stone. Make of this [*mūrti* made of] stone of your own body.

(*Atharva Veda*, 2.13.4)

At more advanced levels, *arcana* can be performed as *mānasa-pūjā*, which is mental worship carried out without any ritual or external object. In this case, devotees visualize the entire ceremony internally, offering a seat to the Lord on the altars of their hearts. This type of ritual is only feasible for those who have performed puja for several years and who are familiar with the order of the offerings. It is possible to combine the *mūrti-pūjā* with *mānasa-pūjā* by making offerings with body and mind.

The dharma shastras, "treatises on duty," also expressly recommend puja. The rich and varied ritual aspect of bhakti yoga forms an integral part of the *Sanātana-dharma* religion.

Aspects and components of worship

According to the *Pañca-rātras*, worship before the deity is incomplete if any of the following five aspects (*pañcāṅga-pūjā*) are excluded:

1. *Abhigamana*, "approaching the temple." This refers to our preparation for worship. It includes properly bathing and cleaning, dressing in clean and appropriate clothes, and decorating the body with tilak. It is connected to the cleaning and decoration of the temple.
2. *Upādāna*, "gathering the articles for worship." This includes collecting fresh flowers, preparing delicious food, selecting proper utensils, and fundraising for temple maintenance, without which worship of the deity would be impossible.
3. Yoga, "establishing oneself in one's own identity." In this context, yoga refers to the repetition of

mantras with a *mālā* and dhyana, or "meditation." *Mānasa-pūjā* is also considered yoga.

4. *Ijyā*, "worship of the Lord," refers to the offering of the different *upacāras*, or "offerings."
5. *Svādhyāya*, "study of the sacred scriptures." In *mūrti* worship, a deep understanding of the rituals is very important so that ignorance does not turn spirituality into a kind of superstition.

The sixteen fundamental components of the basic form of worship, or "*ṣoḍaśopacāra-pūjā*," are as follows:

1. *Āvāhana*, "invocation, invitation." This is performed by reciting mantras that correspond to the specific aspect of God being worshipped. Ultimately, this refers to the awakening of the divinity that dwells in the depths of one's own self.
2. Asana, "seat." This refers to welcoming God and offering him a seat in the deity to whom we offer our ceremony. In a deeper sense, it means offering our own heart as the seat of the Lord.
3. *Pādya*, "bathing the feet" of the *mūrti* with water. Water represents the tears of ecstasy that pure devotees shed when listening to the sacred name of God. *Pādya* means bathing the lotus feet of the Lord with the waters of our devotion.
4. *Arghya*, offering "water to the hands" of the Lord. It is the symbol of our surrender into the hands of God.
5. *Ācamana*, offering "sipping water" to the deity. It is the offering of our sincere devotion to the Lord.

6. *Snāna*, ceremonial "bathing" of the *mūrti*. The most profound meaning of the act of bathing the deity is connected to our own cleanliness and purification. When we have been cleansed of all that is earthly and mundane within us, our divine nature will be revealed.
7. *Vastra*, "garments." The offering of beautiful, spotless clothing to the Lord.
8. *Upavīta*, "sacred thread." The offering of the sacred thread.
9. *Vilepana*, "anointing." The anointing of the deity with turmeric or sandalwood ointment.
10. *Puṣpāñjali*, "two handfuls of flowers." The offering of flowers and garlands.
11. *Dhūpa*, "incense." Incense symbolizes the fragrance that emanates from our ego when it is burned as an offering to the Lord.
12. *Dīpa*, "lamp." Offering the light from a ghee lamp, one of the most sacred symbols of the *Sanātana-dharma* religion.
13. *Naivedya*, "food offering" of delicious food and sweets to the deity.
14. *Nīrājana*, an offering that involves moving a lit camphor lamp in circles in front of the *mūrti*.
15. *Mantra-puṣpa* is to offer red, uncooked rice, turmeric, and flowers while all devotees present chant Vedic mantras.
16. *Pradakṣiṇa-namaskāra*, "circumambulation and reverences." Walking in circles around the deity and offering humble reverences.

It is recommended to meditate for thirty minutes (dhyana) before beginning the puja. According to tradition, one should not eat for at least two hours prior to the puja. The *pūjaka* bathes and dresses in clean clothes to approach the Divine. The ritual begins by offering humble reverence to one's spiritual master, previous acharyas in the line of disciplic succession, and finally, to God. This order has been established because, from the devotee's point of view, it is by the guru's mercy that we draw nearer to God. We proceed to glorify all of them with hymns and auspicious mantras, then continue with the invocation (*āvāhana*) through the corresponding mantras of the divine aspect we are worshipping. We then offer the deity an asana (place to sit), followed by *pādya* (washing its feet), *arghya* (washing its hands), *ācamana* (sipping water), *mukhe* (washing its face), and finally *snāna* (bathing the deity).

Next, the deity is dressed (*vastra*) by offering the sacred thread (*upavīta*) for masculine deities and a shawl for feminine deities. Depending on the deity, it is anointed (*vilepana*) with turmeric, sandalwood, etc., then decorated with jewels and flower garlands (*puṣpāñjali*). The deity's 108 names are repeated, and incense (*dhūpa*) and a flame (*dīpa*) are offered. Afterward, *naivedya* (savory dishes and sweets prepared especially for the Divine) is offered. Finally, the bhaktas purify themselves by consuming the remains of the offering called *prasāda* (holy remains of the Lord) with deep reverence.

Next they wash the deity's hands, feet, and face and offer *tāmbūla*, or a "mixture of betel nut and leaves," to refresh, and then the flame from a camphor lamp (*nīrājana*) is waved. All who are present offer rice and flowers (*mantra-puṣpa*) and circumambulate the deity (*pradakṣiṇa*). Finally, the bhaktas offer obeisances (*namaskāra*) and plead forgiveness for any offense they may have committed.

Worship at home

Puja can be performed either in the temple (*mandira*) or at home.

Learning how to perform Vedic *arcana* correctly or to become an expert *pūjaka* can take many years of intensive study, because one must learn the specific mantras for each phase of the many rituals and master their strict rules.

While deity worship at home with the family and friends is less demanding than in the temple, it is no less ecstatic.

ayaṁ svasty-ayanaḥ panthā
dvi-jāter gṛha-medhinaḥ
yac chraddhayāpta-vittena
śuklenejyeta pūruṣaḥ

> The most suitable course for the twice-born householder is the worship of the Lord through sacrifices, using wealth gained honorably.
> (*Bhāgavata Purana*, 10.84.37)

Dedicating a room in the house exclusively for spiritual activities is highly recommended. Decorating this room with pictures of one's spiritual master and the many

Hindu saints and sages will create a meditative and inspirational atmosphere. Aside from serving as a place for meditation, pujas and prayer, it will radiate positive vibrations throughout the entire home and in every member of the family.

The *mūrti*

A *mūrti* is an image that represents God or one of his aspects, incarnations, or manifestations in a concrete form on the physical plane. The word *mūrti* means "manifestation" and refers to that which adopts a specific form. As a specific point upon which to fix one's attention, the *mūrti* encourages prayer and meditation and channels love toward God.

Mūrti-śilpa-śāstra, "ancient Vedic iconography," is considered a sacred art. In order to craft a *mūrti*, it is not enough to be a skillful sculptor or a great artist; one must also live a pure and religious life. Moreover, only someone who has obtained spiritual authority through initiation by a guru from a line of disciplic succession within the *Mūrti-śilpa-śāstra* can craft a *mūrti*.

The task of the *śilpī*, "Vedic sculptor," is difficult because of the absence of a visual model. The *mūrti* is not a fanciful artistic creation produced by the imagination of the sculptor. Rather, it is based on a dhyana shloka, "meditative verse," from the sacred scriptures that describes the manifestation of the divinity that the *śilpī* wishes to sculpt. The sculptor meditates upon the dhyana shloka and prays to God to reveal himself in the desired form.

The *mūrti* is composed of various materials that are described in the *Śilpa-śāstras*. Traditionally, white marble is used in northern India, while black granite is preferred in the south; sometimes metals such as bronze are also utilized. *Mūrtis* are also crafted with *pañca-loha*, a mixture of five metals: gold, silver, brass, copper, and iron. They represent the harmony between the five elements: air, water, fire, earth, and ether. Wooden *mūrtis* are rare and found only in two Indian temples: Trivikrama, in Tirukkoilur, and the famous temple of Lord Jagannātha, in Purī.

Mūrtis that are permanently installed in temples are called *acala* (immovable) or, in Tamil, *dhruva-bera* (immobile image), and are typically sculpted from granite or marble. There are three classes of *Acala-mūrtis*: *sthānaka* (standing), *āsīna* (seated), and *śayāna* (reclining). They are also grouped by their attitudes: *ugra* (ferocious)—such as Mother Kali or Lord Nṛsiṁhadeva—and *śānta* (serene)—such as their Lordships Rādha-śyāma, Lord Hanuman, and Lord Gaṇeśa.

To become qualified for worship, the *mūrti* must first be installed through a *prāṇa-pratiṣṭhā*, "imparting of life" ceremony. Once installed, it must be treated with the highest respect.

Young people channel their emotions toward famous singers and athletes. To nurture inspiration toward their ideals, they decorate their rooms with pictures and posters of these celebrities. In a similar way, devotees receive great spiritual inspiration through the deity as well as a channel that allows them to integrate their emotions. The worship of the *mūrti* is a practical method to invoke the sacred through a specific image. We do not worship the stone, the marble or the image in itself, but we worship God through this image. *Mūrti-pūjā* is not idolatry, because ultimately it is the worship of God.

The attitude of the bhakti yogi

The quality of the puja is not determined by offerings but our love in offering them. Without devotion, worship is at risk of losing its religious and spiritual value, and becoming merely a social custom.

As Lord Krishna declares:

patraṁ puṣpaṁ phalaṁ toyaṁ
yo me bhaktyā prayacchati
tad ahaṁ bhakty-upahṛtam
aśnāmi prayatātmanaḥ

> If one offers me a leaf, a flower, a fruit, or water with love and devotion, I will accept it.
>
> (Bhagavad Gita, 9.26)

In this verse, Krishna does not request money, jewels, precious stones, or objects of great value from us. On the contrary, he assures us that he will accept very simple offerings if they are accompanied with sincere devotion, because the only requisite is love.

The spirit of *arcana* does not aspire to manipulate the divine will or attempt to obtain personal gain or benefits, but only to express love and devotion to God. Thus, we must avoid turning religious ceremonies into a type of spiritual business.

To request personal or even heavenly benefits is the approach of beginners on the spiritual path. Any attempt to bargain with heaven will bring about degeneration in the nature of *arcana*. An immature bhakta who seeks comforts will stagnate in this process, unable to reach the subtler and more abstract levels to which bhakti can lead.

As affirmed by Gauḍapāda:

upāsanāśrito dharmo
jāte brahmaṇi vartate
prāg-utpatter ajaṁ sarvaṁ
tenāsau kṛpaṇaḥ smṛtaḥ

> One who engages in devotional practices (*upāsānā*), while subsisting in the manifest [conditioned] Brahman, is considered pitiable [because he thinks that] before birth [or creation], all was of the same nature as the birthless Brahman [i.e. he believes that birth actually happened and Brahman became conditioned by it].
>
> (*Māṇḍūkya-kārikā*, 3.1)

In his commentary on this verse, Śaṅkarācārya explains it this way:

> *Upāsanāśritaḥ* is a worshipper who turns to *upāsanā*, devotional practices (such as worship and meditation), as a means to liberation, believing that

"I am a worshipper, and Brahman is to be adored by me. Even though I now subsist as *jāte brahmaṇi* in conditioned Brahman, through my devotion to him I shall attain *ajaṁ brahma*, the unconditioned Brahman, after the demise of my body. *Prāg-utpatter ajaṁ sarvam*, before the creation, all this, including myself, was but the birthless Brahman. Through my devotional exercises, I shall regain that which I essentially was before birth, *prāg-utpatteḥ*. However, after having being born, I now subsist in the conditioned Brahman: *jāte brahmaṇi*." The *dharmaḥ*, the aspirant or *upāsanāśritaḥ*, is one who dedicates himself to such devotional exercises, since he or she is thus conscious of Brahman limited by time (*tena*). For that very reason (*asau*), such a person (*smṛtaḥ*) is considered *kṛpaṇaḥ*, or pitiable and limited, by those who have seen the eternal and birthless Brahman. This is the idea. And it is in accordance with the following text of the Upanishad, in the section *talava-kāra* of the *Sama Veda*: "That which is not uttered by speech, that by which speech is revealed, you should know that alone to be Brahman, and not what people worship as an object." (*Kena Upanishad*, 1.5)

According to the above said, the practice of *arcana* does not try to influence the Divine's will with a manipulative attitude, but involves turning to the transcendental and focusing on the way the perception of the worshipper changes.

Thinking that a bhakta is communicating with a marble or bronze statue is like believing a person speaking on the phone is simply conversing with a plastic device. Just as a phone is a means of communication, the deity is merely a channel for our devotion toward God. Similarly, when we kiss a letter from a loved one, we are not expressing love for the paper or ink, but for the person who wrote it. Just as devotees do not limit or reduce God to the deity worshipped in the temple, they consciously accept the deity as a sacred instrument and means to relate directly with the transcendental.

Some may argue that limiting contact with God to a deity confined to a specific place contradicts divinity's omnipresent nature, but this is as absurd as arguing that a handshake greets a hand, not a person. Just as a handshake involves communication with the entire person, deity worship expresses our devotional feelings through contact with a part that represents the Whole. The Lord is omnipresent; his divine presence is everywhere and transcends space. The ancient sages taught that the deity is the compassionate Lord's extended hand. By simply touching it, the bhakta establishes intimate communion with him.

God is present everywhere in the universe and one who experiences him has no need for temples, images, sculptures, or any other external stimuli. However, those who are not yet capable of such a level of consciousness may sincerely and honestly accept that the worship of the *mūrti* can be an aid to invoke the presence of heaven in their hearts.

Believing that we and God are separate entities, we strive to discover the Absolute in the dualistic platform. God is our objectification of Brahman. *Arcana* arises when we try to connect to our true nature as if it were an object.

Puja is a powerful meditation that starts in the world of names and forms, and draws us nearer to both the spiritual master and God. It is an effort to communicate with the spiritual world from the physical plane, an attempt to contact the transcendental from the relative, the Absolute from the dual.

When we meditate with closed eyes, we pursue divinity in the very depths of ourselves, but puja reminds us that God also lies in the exterior, and that concepts such as "inside" and "outside" are nothing more than illusory points of reference from which we create imaginary directions.

The worship of God on specific hours and days inside the walls of the temple is just the basic level of *arcana*. Eventually, devotees reach the most elevated level of *arcana* when they offer themselves and their lives as sacrifices on the altars of their hearts.

If this world no longer appears to be a sacred temple, it is because long ago we incorporated it into the known. Living from our past, we turned life into a habit and made our existence a routine. For too long we have stopped being touched by the miracle of existence. How can we attempt to worship God if we are not moved by the blossoming of spring? How can we yearn to venerate the Lord if we are not filled with wonder when looking at the star-filled sky?

Religious books can explain protocol and how to appropriately position ourselves before an altar, but the more advanced levels of *arcana* are reached on an autumn morning in the forest or on a summer evening by the sea. Only the full moon reflecting on a lake can teach the heart to bow low before the creator; nothing less than the majesty of a desert sunset can inspire the soul to offer its most humble and respectful reverences to God.

Through the blessings of *arcana*, our lives become an uninterrupted series of moments of worshipping God. Only then will we reciprocate life by offering it the finest that it has given us: the color of flowers, the radiance of light, the enchantment of melodies, the vibrations of hymns, the perfume of incense, and the freshness of water. When we strive to offer the best of ourselves in every moment, our entire lives are transformed into a puja in this great temple that is the universe.

Vandana, "reverence, prayer"

Vandana refers to prostrations, reverence, and prayer offered to God. When we pray, we invoke the divine aid of Īśvara—the Supreme Controller. Without his support, we can never succeed, even if we strive endlessly. We can only extol the greatness of God and plead for his protection when we recognize our limitations and accept how small we are.

God is impartial, so he lets his grace come down indiscriminately, like rain over all beings. In this sense, praying is like closing our umbrellas and allowing his blessings to soak us.

Like the sun, divine grace radiates to illuminate all. When we pray, we expose ourselves to the warmth and light of God's rays and open our hearts to his benevolence.

Types of prayer

Vandana generally refers to offerings in the form of prayers, which can be divided into three types: (1) through the body (*kāyika*), (2) through speech (*vācika*), and (3) through mental prayer (*mānasika*).

Kāyika-vandana, "bodily prayer," means bowing before the deity or the spiritual master. The reverence that devotees offer is an external expression of the devotion that they experience in their hearts. Bhaktas absorb the spiritual energy that emanates from the deity's or guru's feet when they bow before them and show respect, surrender, and submission.

As devotees mature, these noble sentiments continue to expand until they encompass all beings. Bhakti yogis can recognize their beloved Lord as the one unity lying beyond this reality of names and forms. Perceiving the unity that underlies all diversity, devotees are liberated of any trace of racism or sectarianism, and their expansive spirits are reflected in interactions with others, just as Krishna explains to Uddhava:

visṛjya smayamānān svān
dṛśaṁ vrīḍāṁ ca daihikīm
praṇamed daṇḍavad bhūmāv
ā śva-cāṇḍāla-go-kharam

> Ignoring the ridicule of one's companions, one should renounce the bodily concept of life and its associated embarrassments, and offer reverence to all living beings, even horses, cows, donkeys, and untouchables, completely prostrating one's body upon the ground as straight as a rod.
>
> (*Uddhava-gītā*, *Bhāgavata Purana*, 11.29.16)

A great part of the wisdom that we find in the sacred scriptures was put together in the form of prayers. *Vācika-vandana*, "verbal prayer," refers to the repetition of prayers created by the acharyas of the past.

Many people find it difficult to feel connected with this type of prayer because their attitudes and emotions are not always in harmony with the words that they speak. However, the great benefit of *vācika-vandana* prayers actually resides in the way they attune us to the spiritual experiences of the rishis who wrote them. One might say that when we are unsure of the appropriate words with which to address God, the best thing is to repeat the words of those who knew how to express themselves in front of him.

The third type of prayer is *mānasika-vandana*, "mental prayer." The master and Lord will only accept our *vandana* when it is accompanied by the correct inner attitude. In order to access this type of prayer, one needs higher qualities such as mental purity and internal cleanliness. Thoughts related to the pastimes of the Lord or to our spiritual master can serve to gradually purify our internal world.

Kinds of worshippers and prayers

Krishna states:

catur-vidhā bajante māṁ
janāḥ sukṛtino 'rjuna
ārto jijñāsur arthārthī
jñānī ca bharatarṣabha

> O greatest of the *Bhāratas*, four classes of pious people worship me: those who are afflicted (*ārta*), those who desire wealth (*arthārthin*), seekers of the Truth (*jijñāsu*), and those who have realized the Truth (*jñānī*).
> (Bhagavad Gita, 7.16)

Likewise, four types of devotees pray to God: the *ārta*, the *arthārthī*, the *jijñāsu*, and the *jñānī*. Each recognizes and worships God, but the difference lies in their attitudes. Each type of devotee reflects their level of development and maturity in their prayer.

1. *Ārta-bhakta*: *Ārti* is a Sanskrit word that means "sorrow, pain, and sickness." *Ārta* refers to those who suffer sorrow, such as that caused by theft, a disease, a tragedy, or a tiger attack. *Ārta-bhaktas* are desperate. Feeling vulnerable, they cry out, imploring the Lord for help. They are considered tamasic, and their prayers are a cry for refuge and safety arising from a state of helplessness. It is a plea typically motivated by health problems or urgent needs. At times, certain situations of extreme difficulty make us feel powerless and destitute. It is in these moments that the prayer of *ārta-bhaktas* emerges—it is the cry of a desperate heart.

2. *Arthārthi-bhakta*: In Sanskrit, *artha* means "the desired" and this refers specifically to wealth, power, or progeny. These devotees approach the Supreme Lord seeking family, wealth, and fame. *Arthārthi-bhaktas* are rajasic and when they pray, they ask God for knowledge, status, wealth, power, honor, or fame. Such is the prayer of business owners who seek divine help for their companies. The prayers of *ārtas* and *arthārthins* are among the most common today. Although both are worldly,

when they are faced with adversity, they turn to Īśvara for assistance and consolation. They both have characteristics of devotees because they place confidence in the Supreme Self and not in their own abilities.

3. *Jijñāsu-bhakta*: The word *jijñāsu* in Sanskrit means "one who is desirous of knowledge or wisdom." These devotees are not attracted to what society deems successful, but instead feel the need to investigate the true meaning of life. Although they may have material possessions, *jijñāsu-bhaktas* understand that meaning cannot be reduced solely to sensual pleasure. Their souls perceive the emptiness of a life without spirituality. These devotees are sattvic and highly elevated, because they delve into the very essence of God until they understand the meaning of the *Vedanta Sutra* (1.1.1), *athāto brahma-jijñāsā*, which says, "now is the moment for us to inquire into the Absolute Truth." The prayer of *jijñāsu-bhaktas* emerges from the sincere search for the Truth. These devotees' thirst for God leads to prayers for wisdom and knowledge, imploring the Divine for the grace to overcome any obstacle or weakness produced by ignorance.

4. *Jñāni-bhakta*: These devotees have experienced the authentic essence of Krishna as their own subjectivity; they are sages who have realized God as Parameśvara, the nature that lies in the

depths of everyone and everything. *Jñāni-bhaktas* are enlightened beings and authentic, pure devotees. The highest type of prayer is the prayer of *jñānīs*. It only emanates from enlightened beings who are firmly within divinity, and have transcended the physical body and connected with the light of higher planes of consciousness.

nāhaṁ vande tava caraṇayor dvandvam advandva-hetoḥ
kumbhī-pākaṁ gurum api hare nārakaṁ nāpanetum
ramyā rāmā mṛdu-tanu-latā nandane nāpi rantuṁ
bhāve bhāve hṛdaya-bhavane bhāvayeyaṁ bhavantam

O Lord Hari, I pray to your lotus feet, not to be saved from the duality of existence or to escape from this hell darkened by burning tribulations, nor to enjoy the beautiful soft-skinned women who dwell in the garden of paradise. I pray only that love for you arises from the depths of my heart and in my every thought, birth after birth.

(*Mukunda-mālā Stotra*, 4)

The first three types of devotees try to influence the will of God by praying, imploring, pleading, requesting, and begging. In contrast, the prayer of the forth type, *jnānī-bhaktas*, is meditation, expressing a deep state of communion with the Whole. Truly, what bhaktas experience as prayer, *jnānis* live as meditation.

Prayer rises in quality as greed diminishes. Pure devotees do not pray to God out of repression or to receive personal favors; rather, they are free of desires. They do not plead for wealth because they have given everything to the Lord and no longer need anything. Hence, their prayer does not stem from dissatisfaction; rather, it emanates as a constant internal flow of gratitude toward existence, life, and God.

The prayer of the jivanmukta, or one who is "liberated in life," arises from a meditative heart that has transcended egoism and gone beyond the realm of the mind. In ordinary prayer, people speak to God, whereas in the prayer of enlightened beings, the Divine responds. In this way, it has the magic and fresh fragrance of an encounter with the beloved.

When we situate ourselves in the here and now, we experience reality, love, compassion, bliss, and innocence; the heart overflows with gratitude. Gratitude is the silent prayer of a receptive and sensitive heart, amazed by the miracle of being.

Dāsya, "being the servant of God"

Dāsya means cultivating "an attitude of service" toward God, and thinking of yourself as a loving servant at the full disposal of your divine master twenty-four hours a day. Devotees surpass the sensation that God belongs to them and experience that, in fact, they belong to the Lord.

The Lord describes actions favorable to cultivating devotion to Uddhava, among which he mentions the following:

ādaraḥ paricaryāyāṁ
sarvāṅgair abhivandanam
mad-bhakta-pūjābhyadhikā
sarva-bhūteṣu man-matiḥ

> See me in all living beings, serve me with care and great respect, offer reverence with all bodily limbs, and worship my devotees above all.
>
> (*Bhāgavata Purana*, 11.19.21)

mad-artheṣv aṅga-ceṣṭā ca
vacasā mad-guṇeraṇam
mayy arpaṇaṁ ca manasaḥ
sarva-kāma-vivarjanam

> Offer your mind to me and utterly reject material desires, employing every movement of the limbs for my sake and every word to describe my qualities.
>
> (*Bhāgavata Purana*, 11.19.22)

Cultivation of *dāsya* eradicates selfishness and its expressions, such as arrogance and pride. To live in the spirit of service leads to happiness and a life full of meaning. In the *Bhāgavata Purana* we read the following:

maitreya uvāca
na vai mukundasya padāravindayo
rajo-juṣas tāta bhavādṛśā janāḥ
vāñchanti tad-dāsyam ṛte 'rtham ātmano
yadṛcchayā labdha-manaḥ-samṛddhayaḥ

> Maitreya said: "My dear Vidura, people who are eager to relish [by way of service] the dust of Lord Mukunda's lotus feet have their desires fulfilled automatically [by the Lord's grace]. Considering themselves to be very rich, their only wish is to serve the Lord."
>
> (*Bhāgavata Purana*, 4.9.36)

Loving servants of God can cultivate *dāsya* living in an ashram or in society, because they view the entire universe as the mansion of their Lord. Indeed, *dāsya* does not require us to neglect our daily duties, but invites us to perform our work with the awareness that everything and everybody belongs to the Lord and is controlled by him.

Progress in spiritual life depends essentially on an understanding of *dāsya*. Those who are unable to develop this virtue stagnate in spiritual development, and may even leave the religious path. If we really wish to advance, it is essential to be initiated by a true spiritual master, accept his or her guidance, and see ourselves as a servant to our master, our spiritual brothers and sisters, our mission, humanity, and God.

In a class-based society, servants are viewed as those who lack the training, resources, or skills to seek a better position. However, manifold qualities are required to fulfill the duties of a servant to someone great: the personal assistant to a president or a king will never be someone ordinary. Similarly, to become a servant of God, one must develop the highest virtues, such as purity, compassion, love, and devotion.

As humility develops, we will understand that it is presumptuous even to aspire to be accepted as a servant of God. Therefore, it is a great privilege to be initiated by a spiritual master who can connect us to a chain of disciplic succession and in this way, be accepted as the servant of a servant of a servant of a servant of God.

nāhaṁ vipro na ca nara-patir nāpi vaiśyo na śūdro
nāhaṁ varṇī na ca gṛha-patir no vana-stho yatir vā
kintu prodyan-nikhila-paramānanda-pūrṇāmṛtābdher
gopī-bhartuḥ pada-kamalayor dāsa-dāsānudāsaḥ

> I am not a *Brāhmaṇa*, a Kshatriya, a Vaishya, or a Sudra. I am not a brahmachari, a grihastha, a vanaprastha, or a sannyasi. I am just a servant of a servant of a servant of the lotus feet of the Lord, who is the supporter of the *gopīs*, ever brilliant, an ocean of nectar and the eternal cause of universal transcendental bliss.
>
> (*Śrī-caitanya-caritāmṛta*, "*Madhya-līlā*," 13.80)

Servants of the Lord can be divided into four categories:

1. *Adhikṛta-dāsa*, "appointed servant": Devas who have assumed particular responsibilities and specific missions within the manifested universe, such as Lord Brahma, Lord Shiva, Indra, Kali, and Durgā.
2. *Āśrita-dāsa*, "sheltered servant": Devotees such as Śaunaka, Harihara, Bahulāśva, and Ikṣvāku who have taken refuge and found shelter under the lotus feet of the Lord. They feel that there is no security besides God's and know that only he can offer true protection.
3. *Pāriṣada-dāsa*, "companion servant": Trustworthy and loyal devotees who perform personal service to the Lord, such as Uddhava, Dāruka, Hanuman, and Sātyaki.
4. *Anugata-dāsa*, "accompanying servant": These are the most intimate servants of the Lord within Vraja (Vrindavana and Mathura) and Dvārakā, and their hearts are always absorbed in affectionate service to the Lord. Krishna's close servants Citraka, Raktaka, Bakula, Śārada, Sucandra, and Maṇḍana are examples of these servants.

The values of a materialistic society assume that servants are in a lower position because they enjoy less freedom, appreciation, and pay. It is considered a sign of success to have many servants, so it is not surprising that the idea of becoming a servant does not inspire most people. No one wishes to serve; on the contrary, most people try to control others out of their own selfish interests. If we aspire to be servants of the Lord, we must undergo a complete reversal of our attitudes, cease being consumers and become contributors.

Dāsya entails letting go of our fear of being exploited and having the willingness to dedicate everything to God; it involves replacing a craving to possess with the longing to be possessed; it means no longer desiring control, but solely wishing to make ourselves accessible.

While *pāda-sevanan* means being engaged in serving the Lord, *dāsyam* means no longer belonging to ourselves but to God. Devotees who have committed themselves in *dāsyam* move away from what the Lord dislikes and direct their actions toward all that their owner approves of. They are no longer guided by their own reason or will. They no longer satisfy selfish appetites and interests. They have learned to not belong to themselves and to live only for God; every aspect of their existence is directed toward him.

When they stop thinking of themselves as independent, devotees become divine and part of something much greater. In this self-denial, they open themselves up to being a possession of the Absolute. As we progress in *dāsya*, we give up our anxiety for enjoyment from others. We abandon ourselves to the bliss of being God's delight, who is the original, true enjoyer.

Sakhya, "friendliness"

Sakhya is translated as "friendship," but it actually refers to "friendliness." Friendship is relative, since it is meant for a friend, but friendliness is absolute, as it does not depend on anyone. Rather than building a relationship, *sakhya* means cultivating a certain quality; it can even be experienced alone because it arises from one's inner depths. Friendliness is like a candle that illuminates whether or not someone is around, or a campfire that emanates heat even if nobody is near.

When two people without friendliness in their hearts establish a relationship, they may at first embrace one another, say beautiful words, and care for each other. In the future, however, they may not even call to wish the other a happy birthday. Likewise, if a person has friends, it is not necessarily a sign that he is friendly; today I may consider someone my friend but tomorrow I may hate him or her. In contrast, friendliness makes no distinction between friends and enemies, because it arises out of love and freedom.

In general, we have friends to escape loneliness; we utilize them to forget the fact that, in reality, we are alone. As long as we continue to consider loneliness a problem, our "friends" will appear to be mere solutions. Only when we cease to flee loneliness and dare to sincerely contemplate it will we discover the treasure of friendliness concealed within solitude.

Because friendship aims to receive some sort of benefit from someone else, it conceals a type of exploitation, be it economic, social, or sexual. On the other hand, friendliness flows from a selfless heart that is truthful, pure, and authentic. Friendliness is nothing more than love without desires, interests, possessiveness, and jealousy.

Only one who has awakened to friendliness can develop a true friendship not only with every human being, but also with animals, flowers, trees, mountains, the moon, the sun, and the stars. If we look closely, perhaps we will see that we are not even truly friendly to ourselves. But when friendliness blossoms, it is expressed in both our relationships and our attitude toward ourselves.

Devotees who have cultivated friendliness have fostered optimal conditions for the revelation of divinity as the eternal friend.

ati-viśvasta-cittasya
vāsudeve sukhāmbudhau
sauhārdena parā prītiḥ
sakhyam ity abhidhīyate

> A great love endowed with an attitude of friendliness, [experienced] by a very faithful devotee of Lord Vāsudeva, the ocean of bliss, is known as *sakhya*.
> (*Hari-bhakti-kalpa-latikā*, 11.1)

Sakhya is found in other religions, such as the Jewish liturgical poem *Yedid Nefesh*, attributed to the Kabbalist Rabbi Elazar ben Moshe Azikri (1533-1600 CE), which refers to God as the "friend of the soul."

In the devotional process, friendliness is essential because only those capable of a love free of personal interest, egoism, and lust can discover the secret of a relationship with the Divine.

aho bhāgyam aho bhāgyaṁ
nanda-gopa-vrajaukasām
yan mitraṁ paramānandaṁ
pūrṇaṁ brahma sanātanam

O boundless good fortune of Nanda Maharaja, the *gopas*, and the rest of the residents of Vraja! Their fortune is immeasurable because the eternally blissful God is their friend.

(*Bhāgavata Purana*, 10.14.32)

sakhayo nitya-sukhinaḥ
svayam prītā nirāśiṣaḥ
vāsudeve 'navarataṁ
prītiṁ kurvanti nirmalām

Ever happy, content, and desiring nothing, the friends of Lord Vāsudeva always cherish a great and pure love toward him.

(*Hari-bhakti-kalpa-latikā*, 11.3)

Lord Krishna himself states:

sa evāyaṁ mayā te 'dya
yogaḥ proktaḥ purātanaḥ
bhakto 'si me sakhā ceti
rahasyaṁ hy etad uttamam

> I have revealed this ancient yoga to you now, for you are my devotee as well as my friend. Indeed, this is a transcendental mystery.
>
> (Bhagavad Gita, 4.3)

Thus, only when friendliness has arisen from the heart can one experience friendship with the Whole, or *sakhya*, the transcendental mystery of friendship with God.

Ātma-nivedana, "surrendering to God"

Ātma-nivedana means "the surrender of oneself to God." It means offering the Lord all that we believe ourselves to be and possess. Surrender is the height of the devotional process; the other eight limbs are only intended to create the basis and foundation for surrender.

In his *Bhakti-sandarbha*, Jīva Gosvāmī classifies *ātma-nivedana* into two categories: ordinary and extraordinary. The former is known as *bhāva-vinā*, "lacking a specific temperament," while the latter is termed *bhāva-vaiśiṣṭya*, "permeated by an intense devotional nectar."

> *tad etad ātma-nivedanaṁ bhāvaṁ vinā bhāva-vaiśiṣṭyena ca dṛśyate.*
>
> There are two types of self-surrender: the first lacks the specific temperament of love, and the second is inspired by loving feelings.
>
> (*Bhakti-sandarbha*, *anuccheda* 309)

Jīva Gosvāmī cites the following verse to illustrate *bhāva-vinā*:

> *martyo yadā tyakta-samasta-karmā*
> *niveditātmā vicikīrṣito me*
> *tadāmṛtatvaṁ pratipadyamāno*
> *mayātma-bhūyāya ca kalpate vai*

> Those who renounce all [worldly] activities and offer themselves to me completely, with an ardent desire to serve, attain liberation from birth and death, and become equal to me [Krishna].
>
> (*Bhāgavata Purana*, 11.29.34)

Devotees become equal to the Self because they not only renounce physical possessions but also mental ones, including ideas and conclusions they have about themselves.

To explain *bhāva-vaiśiṣṭya*, Rukmiṇī Devi speaks in this beautiful verse:

tan me bhavān khalu vṛtaḥ patir aṅga jāyām
ātmārpitaś ca bhavato 'tra vibho vidhehi
mā vīra-bhāgam abhimarśatu caidya ārād
gomāyu-van mṛga-pater balim ambujākṣa

> Therefore, my Lord, I choose you as my husband, and I offer myself as your wife. Please accept me swiftly, my dearest lotus-eyed Lord. Let Śiśupāla never touch the hero's portion, which would be like a jackal stealing a lion's property.
>
> (*Bhāgavata Purana*, 10.52.39)

Surrender should not be confused with defeat, which always implies failure and weakness. People who feel they have no alternative resign and raise their hands or a white flag as a sign of impotence.

In contrast, although bhaktas may possess many promising possibilities, they choose to renounce them all. Only people who are authentic sovereigns of their lives are capable of yielding to the mandate of devotion, and of ceasing to be their own property in order to belong to God. Hence, instead of losing they will gain, because whatever belongs to the Lord also extends to those who surrender to him.

To consecrate oneself to the Lord means placing utmost faith in his grace. The relationship between surrender and grace is so close that the two may be considered identical: without total surrender to divine will, we are unable to receive the grace of the Lord, and paradoxically, his grace is expressed in our lives as the capacity to surrender to him.

Most human beings move within the established limits of the idea of "I." To surrender to God means ceasing *to live* for and through the "I," in order *to be* in and through God. In this sense, our vision of existence changes completely when we cease to be of the world, while still being in the world.

Ātma-nivedana implies much more than relinquishing our senses, body, feelings and mind to the Lord. It is the surrender of oneself, the servant, the worshipper. In reality, we can only renounce concepts, ideas, beliefs, opinions, and conclusions about our identity; we cannot forsake that which is real in us. When we examine it more deeply, we will see that this surrender simply means abandoning an illusion, letting go of a dream.

These are the words of that jnana luminary, Bhagavān Ramaṇa Maharishi:

> There are only two ways: to conquer destiny or to be independent of it. One is to enquire whose this destiny is and to discover that only the ego is bound by it and not the Self, and that the ego is non-existent. The other way is to kill the ego by completely surrendering to the Lord, realizing one's helplessness and saying all the time: "Not I, but Thou, O Lord!" Giving up all sense of "I" and "mine" and leaving it to the Lord to do what he likes with you. Surrender can never be regarded as complete so long as the devotee wants this or that from the Lord. True surrender is the love of God for the sake of love and nothing else, not even for the sake of salvation. In other words, complete effacement of the ego is necessary to conquer destiny, whether you achieve this effacement through Self-enquiry or through *bhakti-mārga*.
>
> (*Day by Day with Bhagavān*)

Renouncing the idea of "I" and the concept of "mine," bhaktas release all feelings of possession. Self-surrender to God is equivalent to *nirvikalpa* samadhi, because it is our extinction as separate beings in order to emerge in absolute consciousness.

Surrender involves a type of death, followed by a rebirth in Truth. What we believe ourselves to be must die if we are to live fully. *Ātma-nivedana* consists in an extinction of the private and particular, and a resurrection into the universal. As Ramaṇa Maharishi said: "The second path is the way of self-surrender, the way of *śaraṇāgati*.

Surrender to the universal and you will be absorbed in the universal."

We live from the past toward the future. Feeling insecure, we attempt to predict what may happen in order to be prepared. However, tomorrow has no real existence: since we can only anticipate what we have already experienced, our speculations are mere projections of the known.

Ātma-nivedana means letting go of fears, concerns, and emotional problems and developing full confidence in life, existence… in God.

By surrendering to the Lord we will be able to situate ourselves in the present and live each moment of our lives conscious of *what is*. When we consecrate ourselves, we are dead to what was and what will be, to the known and the unknown. We are reborn in the reality of the present. We perish as an idea or psychological time to dwell eternally in the here and now.

vapur-ādiṣu yo 'pi ko 'pi vā
guṇato 'sāni yathā-tathā-vidhaḥ
tad ahaṁ tava pāda-padmayor
aham adyaiva mayā samarpitaḥ

> Whatever the situation with respect to my body and worldly conditions, whatever personality I have been given, here and now I dedicate myself to you completely.
>
> (*Stotra-ratna*, 52)

Love involves surrender and, like love, *ātma-nivedana* exerts an immediate transformative power capable of changing our perception of the world in an instant. Surrender does not imply getting rid of objects, but rather giving up certain assumptions; it means abandoning the idea of separation from the Whole and disconnection from the flowers and stars, to wake up to reality. The *Vedanta Sutra* says that we must transcend our fears to penetrate the unknown; *ātma-nivedana* means letting go of the ideas we have developed about ourselves and simply dare to open our eyes and see reality as it is.

Although preparing the appropriate conditions can lengthen the journey, *ātma-nivedana* in itself is nothing more than a simple step out of the mind. It simply means leaving the territory of the ego and the personal to jump into the universal. The path from the human to the Divine is not long; we just must take a small leap: from ignorance to wisdom, from pain to bliss, from the relative to the Absolute, the temporal to the eternal, the darkness of the ego to the light of divinity.

CHAPTER 6

Devotional Joy

The bhakti doctrine is an integral part of *Sanātana-dharma*. It is considered the simplest of the four classic paths to liberation since it facilitates direct access to God through love. It became popular among people of all origins because it has no prior requirements and makes possible a personal and intimate relationship with the Almighty without any intermediary. Indian civilization is characterized by including a large variety of voices that may appear to be in conflict. The bhakti movement is an excellent example of Hinduism's culture of unity in diversity and its rich cultural heritage.

Bhakti goes back to the roots of Indian civilization, appearing in Vedic hymns, and was then developed over many generations until reaching its peak during the Middle Ages. Medieval bhakti was stimulated by the translation of Sanskrit writings to local languages and a new wave of devotion to a personal God. This movement expanded from southern India northward, and then to Bengal, Maharashtra, Kashmir, Gujarat, and Assam.

Sri Chaitanya Mahāprabhu (1486-1533 CE) popularized bhakti in Bengal through the *Gauḍīya*

Vaishnava school and established social reforms. Sri Chaitanya ignored all class distinctions and included all castes and communities in his movement. He also believed in fraternity and equality. Proof of this is that his closest disciple, Haridāsa, was one of many with Islamic roots.

Vaishnavism became popular thanks to the endeavors of Sri Chaitanya. His devotion led him to states of ecstasy, crying, and even fainting when chanting the *mahā-mantra* while dancing with his disciples and associates. The masses felt drawn to the holiness and nectar that radiated from his devotional experience. His teachings were based on the adoration of Krishna and his consort Rādhā.

This great saint of Bengal spread Krishna bhakti, "devotion to Krishna," throughout India and popularized the practice of *saṅkīrtana*, "devotional group singing," accompanied by ecstatic dancing.

The only written legacy of Sri Chaitanya was a poem of eight verses, or shlokas, called *Śikṣāṣṭaka*. He delegated the responsibility of structuring his teaching to a very select group of intimate disciples known as the *gosvāmīs* of Vrindavana, who created a religious order in Mathura, India. Not only were they great enlightened masters, but also learned scholars. Six of them were of the *Brāhmaṇa* class and knew Sanskrit; they reorganized caste restrictions and compiled devotional practices. These were the eloquent masters of bhakti yoga who firmly established the teachings of Sri Chaitanya through their writings. They explained his message in detail for the benefit of all humanity. Among the most notable figures, we have Jīva Gosvāmī, author of the

Sat-sandharbas; Sanātana Gosvāmī, author of *Hari-bhakti-vilāsa*; and Rūpa Gosvāmī, whose extraordinary work was the *Bhakti-rasāmṛta-sindhu.*

The ocean of nectarean devotion

The *Bhakti-rasāmṛta-sindhu*, "the ocean of nectarean devotion," is a detailed and systematic study of human emotions and feelings. The author used terms from Hindu aesthetic theory, which is the philosophic discipline that studies the conditions of beauty in art and nature. In this way, the author gave form to a religious-aesthetic theory and offered a new perspective on religion that remains influential today.

Emotional agitation is considered an obstacle to spiritual evolution, which requires tranquility. Considering the need for emotional peace, many disciplines in India recommend repressing emotions. However, within India's pluralism there are traditions that, while agreeing uncontrolled emotions are problematic, maintain they can be quite useful in spiritual life under certain conditions. They argue that feelings are too powerful and potentially effective to be ignored.

In the *Bhakti-rasāmṛta-sindhu*, Rūpa Gosvāmī offers a path different from ascetic repression and explains how emotional activity helps initiate a relationship with God. He even goes further to affirm that love for God consists of the essence of all emotion and is a manifestation of divinity. Instead of repressing feelings, he suggests cultivating them and directing them toward Krishna, as they are an effective means of creating a relationship with the supreme divine lover. Clearly, this path requires a detailed analysis of emotions and a rigorous study of feelings. Hence, this work presents a yoga of divine or spiritual emotions.

The wise men of India have passed down their insightful observations on sensitivity. Going deeper into the Hindu worldview will help us understand our emotional activity, observe it, and finally transcend it. This brings us to the profoundly religious world of *Gauḍīya* Vaishnavism, as conceived by Rūpa Gosvāmī. The principal aspiration is the experience of *rasa*, which refers to the culmination of the joy of a divine emotion. Rūpa Gosvāmī's ideas on *rasa* are better understood in the context of the other debates on this concept. Reflections on the nature and experience of *rasa* have had a long and fascinating history in India.

The Sanskrit word *rasa* literally means "juice, knowledge, or taste" and can be translated as "nectar." Although the term *rasa* is frequent in Vedic literature, its meaning can vary depending on the context. In the Vedas, the word *rasa* is mentioned many times as "liquid," referring to the sacred Vedic rituals. For example, the *Rig Veda* (9.63.13) mentions *soma-rasa*, which is juice of the *soma* plant offered in sacrifices called *soma-yāgas*. In other hymns from the *Rig Veda*, such as 8.72.13, *rasa* refers to liquids like water or milk, and in 5.44.14 it refers to the essence of milk. As for the Upanishads, such as the *Bṛhad-āraṇyaka*, the term *rasa* indicates prana and in the *Taittirīya* (1.3.19) it means "ultimate reality."

The concept of *rasa* inherited by Rūpa emerged in the specific context of aestheticism, specifically in reflections on the nature of dramatic experience. In this field, the term *rasa* is better translated as "dramatic sentiment" or "aesthetic enjoyment." The masters of *Gauḍīya* Vaishnavism used artistic elements to communicate their devotional theology of Krishna bhakti.

Rūpa Gosvāmī's theory of *rasa* was mainly enriched by three prior theories:

1. Bharata Muni's theory of *rasa* (lived sometime between the fifth century BCE to the third century CE): He was an ancient Hindu dramatist, musician, and author of the *Nāṭya-śāstra*, a theoretical treatise on classic drama, specifically Sanskrit theater.
2. Abhinavagupta's theory of *rasa* (950–1020 CE): This renowned follower of Shiva born in Kashmir was a polymath, philosopher, and a mystic. Known widely as a wise man and recognized for his notable influence in Indian culture, he was also an esteemed musician, poet, playwright, analyst, and theologian.
3. King Bhoja's theory of *rasa* (Reigned from early 1000-1055 CE): Bhoja was a philosopher king and scholar who reigned over Central India's Kingdom of Mālava during the Medieval Era.

Bharata Muni's theory of *rasa*

Bharata Muni's *Nāṭya-śāstra* was one of the first treatises on Hindu music, dance, and drama. It is so important that it is traditionally considered the fifth Veda. It was the first recognized text in which the theory of *rasa* was developed in relation to theatrical art.

Bharata condensed the meaning of the multifaceted word *rasa* in a single phrase:

atrāha— rasa iti kaḥ padārthaḥ? ucyate— āsvādyatvāt.

> What is the meaning of the word *rasa*? It is said: due to its quality of being tasted.
>
> (*Nāṭya-śāstra*, 6.31)

In the first chapter of the *Nāṭya-śāstra*, the wise Bharata describes how the God Brahma created this science:

jagrāha pāṭhyam ṛg-vedāt
sāmabhyo gītam eva ca
yajur-vedād abhinayān
rasān ātharvaṇād api

> [Brahma] did this by taking words from the *Rig Veda*, music from the *Sāma Veda*, movements from the *Yajur Veda*, and *rasas* from the *Atharva Veda*.
>
> (*Nāṭya-śāstra*, 1.17)

In the sixth chapter, sages ask Bharata to describe

bhāvas and *rasas* in detail, among other theatrical topics. Bharata responds:

> *tatra rasān eva tāvad ādāv abhivyākhyāsyāmaḥ. na hi rasād ṛte kaścid arthaḥ pravartate.*
>
> Of these topics, we will first explain what *rasas* are, because without *rasa*, no dramatic performance can attract an audience.
>
> (*Nāṭya-śāstra*, 6.31)
>
> *harṣādīṁś cādhigacchanti. tasmān nāṭya-rasā ity abhivyākhyātāḥ.*
>
> [Through these *rasas*, spectators] become happy and so forth, therefore, they are called *nāṭya-rasas*.
>
> (*Nāṭya-śāstra*, 6.31)

Of the great variety of human emotions, Bharata recognized eight principal ones and called them *sthāyi-bhāvas*. The Sanskrit word *sthāyi* means "permanent, constant, and durable" and *bhāva* is derived from the root *bhū*, "to be." *Bhāva* literally means "transform, to be, or a form of being" and is often used to denote a mood, emotion, or feeling. Later, this author clearly described the triggers (*vibhāvas*) that stimulate and release each *sthāyi-bhāva*, the physical reactions (*anubhāvas*) that come from experiencing each *sthāyi-bhāva*, and how they are intensified by the temporary feelings (*vyabhicāri-bhāvas*) and physical manifestations (*sāttvika-bhāvas*) that accompany them.

- ***Sthāyi-bhāvas*** are fundamental emotional dispositions, enduring and constant. Upon being experienced, they absorb us in such a way that neutralizes the rest of our feelings and take all importance or relevance from them. Vedic wise men have recognized eight *sthāyi-bhāvas*: love (*rati*), laughter (*hāsa*), affliction (*śoka*), anger (*krodha*), vitality (*utsāha*), fear (*bhaya*), disgust (*jugupsā*), and awe (*vismaya*).
- ***Vibhāvas*** are stimuli that trigger emotions and cause the various *sthāyi-bhāvas* to manifest. Some examples are sounds, gestures, and so forth.
- ***Anubhāvas*** are expressions or indications that a certain *sthāyi-bhāva* is being experienced. *Anu* in Sanskrit means "after or posterior" and *bhāva* is "emotion," so the *anu-bhāvas* are "reactions to emotions" or the results of the intensification of *sthāyi-bhāvas.* They comprise a great variety of physical gestures, tones of voice, and so forth.
- ***Vyabhicāri-bhāvas*** are temporal emotions of lower intensity that complement the *sthāyi-bhāvas.* The word *vyabhicāri* is the antonym of *sthāyi.* While *sthāyi* means "permanent or fundamental," the prefix *vi* indicates *vividha*, which is "multiple or diverse," so the word *vyabhicārī* means "changeable, irregular, passing, or transitory." There are thirty-three *vyabhicāri-bhāvas.* Some examples are shame, anxiety, and pride.
- ***Sāttvika-bhāvas*** are involuntary physical reactions to specific emotions. The term comes from

> the word sattva because they can manifest in those in whom sattva predominates. When the *sāttvika-bhāvas* manifest, they intensify the *sthāyi-bhāvas* that cause them. There are eight *sāttvika-bhāvas*: astonishment (*stambha*), perspiration (*sveda*), hair standing on end (*romāñca*), broken voice (*svara-bheda*), trembling (*vepathu*), paleness (*vaivarṇya*), tears (*aśru*), and fainting (*pralaya*).

Artistic experience can intensify fundamental emotions, or *sthāyi-bhāvas*, to the point of enjoyment, called *rasa*. The *rasas* are the supreme pleasures tasted when all of the *bhāvas* combine. *Rasa* is a sweetness that is experienced when one of the *sthāyi-bhāvas* combines with its *vibhāvas*, *anubhāvas*, *vyabhicāri-bhāvas*, and *sāttvika-bhāvas*; that is, a *rasa* consists of five types of *bhāvas*: the basic eternal emotion intensified by four types of emotional experiences.

Bharata compares the experience of *rasa* to tasting culinary delicacies. The *sthāyi-bhāvas* are like the basic tastes of sweetness, saltiness, sourness, and bitterness. To perceive these tastes, spices are added, which are like the four emotional experiences: *vibhāva*, *anubhāva*, *vyabhicāri-bhāva*, and *sāttvika-bhāva*. As a result, the taste intensifies until it becomes a delight, or *rasa*. In experiencing a *bhāva*, people suffer from their identification with their emotions of pleasure and pain. But in artistic experience, the combination of the five *bhāva* components make it possible to observe feelings that lead to relishing *rasa*.

Each *sthāyi-bhāva* produces a certain pleasure and a different *rasa*:

Bhāvas	*Rasas*
Rati – love	*Śṛṅgāra-rasa* – erotic pleasure
Hāsa – laughter	*Hāsya-rasa* – fun/ humorous pleasure
Śoka – affliction/ suffering/sorrow	*Karuṇa-rasa* – compassionate pleasure
Krodha – anger	*Raudra-rasa* – furious pleasure
Utsāha – vigor/vitality/ energy/effort	*Vīra-rasa* – heroic pleasure
Bhaya – fear	*Bhayānaka-rasa* – fearful pleasure
Jugupsā – disgust/ repugnancy	*Bībhatsa-rasa* – repulsive pleasure
Vismaya – admiration/ awe	*Adbhuta-rasa* – pleasure of admiration

Theater, for example, integrates various artistic languages and invites us to transcend our private drama to reach a generalized and impersonal experience portrayed by the actors. To achieve such an effect, the audience must put their own stories aside and connect with generic theatrical emotions; spectators cannot enjoy a theatrical performance, a movie, or even a simple soap opera without leaving the confines of their personal emotional constructs.

Rasa is the joy of consciousness relishing itself, seasoned with emotional experiences. Previous experiences are in the mind as latent and unconscious impressions (*vāsanās*). *Rasa* is enjoyed when one of these *vāsanās* is raised to the level of consciousness in a theatrical framework through stimuli (*vibhāvas*) that come from the actors and the scenography, and are later combined with the rest of the *bhāvas*. One example is through the gestures that the actors make (*anubhāvas*). Therefore, *rasa* is the response to an existing feeling in the same way that light reveals a stain that was there before.

To experience *rasa*, people must be open and accessible, become receptive to the stimulus of *rasa*, and remove obstacles that limit consciousness. Aesthetic enjoyment is a special experience of existing emotions. It is tasting without obstacles, a delight without restrictions or limitations. The aesthetic experience of *rasa* is consciousness without the limits of individuality; it is calm contemplation of impersonal emotions. The sensitive observer responds favorably to a situation represented in art, but not in a personal way. The result is an experience totally separated from our ordinary life. We experience the cessation of samsara and its sudden replacement by a new dimension of reality.

Spectators can experience *rasa* when they are free enough to be able to identify with emotions evoked by a situation presented in an artistic representation. No spectator has the same emotional experience as the actors, but rather unconscious impressions (*vāsanās*) similar to the shared background of experiences.

Therefore, aesthetic relishing (*rasa*) does not belong to one person, but is a generalized experience of the *vāsanās*.

A spectator with a refined palate can taste *rasa* when watching a character in a play. These spectators, totally involved and absorbed in the artistic event, experience a potent emotion that is impersonal and generic in nature. *Rasas*, unlike *bhāvas*, are experienced without a direct relationship to the sensitive personal and limited structure. Therefore, in the aesthetic *alaṅkāra*, *rasa* constitutes a state definitively more desired and superior to *bhāva*, because with *rasa*, the one who experiences it accesses a wider spectrum of emotions. At the same time, the impersonal nature of *rasa* protects these spectators from the suffering caused by identifying with pleasurable and painful feelings.

Personal emotions can oscillate between joy and sorrow, happiness and distress. However, even our pleasant feelings cause us pain because they confine us to duality and imprison us in our personal scripts. On the contrary, attentive spectators enjoy all the emotions portrayed on the stage, and because they do not identify with them, they transcend their own misery. Their tears and guffaws are impersonal, and given this distance, they delight even in anger and fear. Emotions cause joy only when they are elevated to a state of *rasa*.

Abhinavagupta's theory of *rasa*

Both the Vaishnava school of poetry in Bengal and its philosophy seem to have been influenced by the teachings of Abhinavagupta, despite not citing him directly.

Abhinavagupta was interested in the close connection between the aesthetic experience and Tantric ritual. He defines *rasa* as the soul of drama and other forms of art, such as poetry.

ānanda-rūpatā sarva-rasānām

The nature of all *rasas* is bliss.

(*Abhinava-bhāratī*, 1.292)

According to Abhinavagupta, the experience of aesthetic *rasa* is similar to that of spiritual *rasa*, because when spectators immerse themselves in the impersonal emotions of the artistic process, they completely forget themselves; the intention is to break the egoistic shell and let the Supreme Self, who naturally identifies with everything and everyone, flow. Similarly, spiritual aspirants abandon their personal dramas and erase the sensitive limits of the "I" to let the generic experience of Brahman occur.

Bhaṭṭa Nāyaka, a writer from Kashmir from the tradition of non-dualism, was probably the first to explain the aesthetic experience in terms of spectators' inner experience. He inspired Abhinavagupta to explore the close relationship between aesthetic and religious experiences and suggested that *rasa* is similar—although not identical—the relishing (*āsvāda*) the Supreme Brahman and compared *rasa* with yogic ecstasy. He believed that theater had a special power to remove the thick layer of ignorance that covers our consciousness and to universalize the emotional situation presented on stage.

According to Abhinavagupta, the aesthetic experience of *rasa* is characterized by pure contemplation dissociated from any personal interest and can bring calm (*viśrānti*). In this way, it is similar to a mystic experience (*brahmāsvāda*). Entering into the depths of a play's world, spectators transcend individual limits and reach the same fusion of the Vedantic mystics. Moreover, both experiences foster transcending the limits of time and space to relish bliss (*ānanda*). Hence, he adds a ninth *rasa* called *śānta-rasa*, "the sweetness of tranquility," with the corresponding *bhāva* of *śama*, "stillness," which is connected to *tattva-jñāna* (knowledge of the Truth) or *ātma-jñāna* (knowledge of the Self), with its principal characteristic being the absence of emotions. Abhinavagupta believes that *śānta-rasa* is the principal *rasa* and that the eight identified by Bharata Muni lead to *śānta-rasa*. It is superior, as it belongs to an elevated plane of peace (*śānti* or *viśrānti*) and, therefore, is not only an aesthetic experience, but also a spiritual one.

However, Abhinavagupta notes important differences. First, an aesthetic experience is temporary and only lasts during the play; returning to their respective worlds, the lives of the spectators do not undergo any radical change. The spiritual moksha experience is deeper and brings drastic changes that transform into permanent characteristics of life. Second, moksha transcends illusions, while the aesthetic experience is part of the illusion because it depends on the emotional content in the unconscious mind of the individual (*vāsanās*) that were acquired from personal experiences.

Illusion is private; reality is universal. A dream, for example, is a private reality: we cannot invite our friends to our dream, nor could they know what we experience while we sleep. Dreams, fantasies, and illusions are private and subjective, but reality is impersonal, generic, universal, and objective. As long as we move within our own personal drama, we remain in a world of theories and hypotheses. Only by opening ourselves to the universal will we find ourselves in the reality of facts. In enlightenment, the limits of personal history are left behind and personal stories are surpassed. This great luminary of Hinduism recognized a means to liberation in art, which helps us transcend, at least temporarily, the consciousness of the ordinary state of wakefulness. In this way, time, and space are transcended, together with the personal nature of emotions. It seems that these teachings inspired Rūpa Gosvāmī to incorporate artistic elements into the devotional path.

King Bhoja's theory of *rasa*

In Rūpa Gosvāmī's rhetoric, we can see the direct influence of Bharata, Dhanañjaya, Śāradātanaya, Siṅgha Bhūpāla, and other authors. However, the most prominent influence is that of Bhoja Raja. For this reason, it is important to present the basic idea of his theory of *rasa*.

King Bhoja governed Mālava (Rajastán) in the eleventh century and had great influence on the medieval world of Sanskrit aesthetics. Like Bhaṭṭa Lollaṭā and Daṇḍin, Bhoja explains that *rasa* is the intensification of a *sthāyi-bhāva*. *Rasa* is produced when a *sthāyi-bhāva* combines with the other components: *vibhāvas*, *anubhāvas*, *vyabhicāri-bhāvas*, and *sāttvika-bhāvas*. Hence, *sthāyi-bhāvas* and *rasas* are one and the same in essence, but differ in levels of intensity and development.

Another important element in Bhoja's theory is that all *rasas* are in fact one. He believes that *śṛṅgāra-rasa* (erotic delight) is the unifying and essential *rasa* that underlies all experiences of pleasure. Likewise, love is the foundation of all aesthetic delight. The other *rasas*, ultimately, are not different from *śṛṅgāra*, but instead are variations.

Like Abhinavagupta, Bhoja maintains that the capacity to experience *rasas* depends on the *vāsanās* of each person. However, he reduces it to just the *vāsanās* that come from performing sacrifices and religious ceremonies prescribed by *Sanātana-dharma*.

This theory differs in a number of aspects from Abhinavagupta's, but Rūpa Gosvāmī seems to have been enriched by both.

The principal influence on Rūpa Gosvāmī's theory of *bhakti-rasa* is that love, or *rati*, is the basis for all the *bhāvas*. When *rati* combines with the other components of *rasa*, it is expressed as different forms of love. This is the position expressed in the *Agni Purana*, a scripture that probably reached its final form in Bengal in the 12th century, and was certainly known and cited by Rūpa Gosvāmī.

Abhinavagupta's theory of *rasa*	Bhoja Raja's theory of *rasa*
Orthodox.	Not orthodox.
The experience of *rasa* is the contemplation of impersonal emotions.	The experience of *rasa* is intensely emotional and personal.
A temporary loss of personal consciousness and generalized experience of an emotion by identifying with a theatrical performance.	Personal identification is elevated to identify with the situation of an actor.
Rasa is the absence of personal emotions.	*Rasa* is the intensification of emotions.
Rasa is a general experience and does not belong to anyone in particular.	*Rasa* is a personal experience resulting from identifying with the actors.
Detachment and distancing are the fundamental requirements for experiencing *rasa*.	Attachment and identification are the requirements for experiencing *rasa*.

Abhinavagupta's theory of *rasa*	**Bhoja Raja's theory of *rasa***
Only people in the audience can experience *rasa*.	Originally, actors experience *rasa*, but if people in the audience have similar *vāsanās* and are able to identify with the actors, they can also experience *rasa*.
The *vāsanās* necessary to experience the *rasas* are shared by everyone.	The *vāsanās* that allow the authentic experience of *rasa* are only those created by religious activities.
The manifestation of *rasa* differs radically from that of *sthāyi-bhāvas*.	The experience of *rasa* is the intensification of *sthāyi-bhāvas*.
Śānta-rasa (tranquility) is the predominant *rasa* that manifests when one has transcended the ordinary emotional experience.	*Śṛṅgāra-rasa* (erotic *rasa*) is the predominant *rasa* and the culmination of the intensification of the emotional experience.
Bhakti is not a separate *rasa* but an emotion that leads to the experience of *śānta-rasa*.	Love, or *rati*, is the basis of all aesthetic pleasure. The other *rasas*, ultimately, are not different from *śṛṅgāra*, but instead are variations.

Rūpa Gosvāmī's theory of *bhakti-rasa*

Rūpa Gosvāmī's theory of *bhakti-rasa* introduces us to devotional delight. The notion of *bhakti-rasa* was known previously, but Rūpa was the first to analyze it in a detailed and systematic way. Although Abhinavagupta included bhakti in his discussions of *rasa*, he did not present it as a separate *rasa*, but instead as an emotion that leads to the tranquility of *śānta-rasa*. The true pioneer in recognizing bhakti as its own *rasa* seems to have been Vopadeva, a writer from thirteen-century Marāthī, India. In his work *Muktāphala*, he presents the first known integral interpretation of bhakti as *rasa*. He accepts the list of nine *sthāyi-bhāvas* and establishes nine types of devotees, each associated with a *rasa* (Bharata's eight in addition to *śānta-rasa*). However, he does not offer a detailed analysis, but simply illustrates each type of *rasa* with citations from the *Bhāgavata Purana*.

mallānām aśanir nṛṇāṁ nara-varaḥ strīṇāṁ smaro mūrtimān
gopānām sva-jano'satāṁ kṣiti-bhujāṁ śāstā sva-pitroḥ śiśuḥ
mṛtyur bhoja-pater virāḍ aviduṣāṁ tatvaṁ paraṁ yogināṁ
vṛṣṇīnāṁ para-devateti vidito raṅgaṁ gataḥ sāgrajaḥ

O king! Sri Krishna, who is the reservoir of all *rasas*, the spring of all divine nectar, was seen in different ways by those who were involved in different relationships with him. When Krishna entered the arena of Kaṁsa accompanied by his older brother, Balarāma, he was seen according

> to the respective mentality of each viewer: to the heroic athletes he seemed like a thunderbolt; the average person saw him as a superhuman, the ladies saw him as the god of love. In the spirit of friendship, the cowherds saw him as their own kinsman. The evil monarchs saw him as a strict ruler and dispenser of justice; his parents saw him as a child. Kaṁsa saw him as death personified. Worldly people saw him as the universal form. The *śānta-rasa* yogis saw him as the supreme soul, the supreme principle, and the Vṛṣṇis saw him as the supreme deity.
>
> (*Bhāgavata Purana*, 10.43.17)

Hemādri expanded on the work begun by Vopadeva in his commentary on the *Muktāphala* called *Kaivalyadīpikā*. In this text, Hemādri maintains that a *rasa* is an intensified *bhāva* and defines a devotee who experiences *bhakti-rasa*. Even though the explanation is not extensive, Hemādri applies various components of Bharata's *rasa-sūtra* to Vaishnava bhakti. Emotions directed toward Vishnu are the means of reaching him. Such emotions are the *sthāyi-bhāvas* of *bhakti-rasa*. Vishnu and his devotees are the foundational stimulators (*ālambana vibhāvas*) of *bhakti-rasa* and things related to Vishnu are the driving stimulators (*uddīpana vibhāvas*). The *anubhāvas* and *vyabhicāri-bhāvas* are applied to the devotees of Vishnu. Hemādri did not present *bhakti-rasa* in a detailed way, but Rūpa Gosvāmī clearly knew his work and was inspired by it.

Another figure that came before Rūpa and seems to have had some influence on him was Lakṣmīdhara. He was most likely a Brahman from Telaṅga who lived between the 13th and 14th centuries, and composed the work *Nāma-kaumudī*. Lakṣmīdhara connected bhakti with *sthāyi-bhāva rati*, "love," and described it as a pleasurable state in which the mind spontaneously concentrates on the Lord. In this way, he established a precedent for the identification of *Kṛṣṇa-rati* as the *sthāyi-bhāva* of *bhakti-rasa*. Hence, it is evident that Rūpa Gosvāmī received the seeds of a long history of debates on bhakti as *rasa*. However, the notions he inherited were not completely developed.

Bhakti is useful as an emotional bridge between the world and the transcendental, and as such makes it possible to reformulate the sensual framework of aesthetic *rasa* based on a devotional attitude. Impregnated with aesthetic sensibility, the nectar of *bhakti-rasa* spills over the limits of art (secular) and rituals (religious). Chanting the holy names of the Lord and listening to his glorious pastimes, *Kṛṣṇa-rati* transforms into *bhakti-rasa* and becomes consciously enjoyable. Bhakti is a conscious process that reveals our hidden nature, which is love.

It is important to understand the difference between *rasa* and *bhakti-rasa*. First, Bharata's classic theory of *rasa* recognizes eight fundamental emotions and a ninth that was added later. But Rūpa believes that all genuine *rasas* are based in one way or another on love for Krishna. On this point, he differs from all other previous theories of bhakti, such as that of Vopadeva, and is closer to the point of view of Bhoja, who reduced all the *rasas* to one called *śṛṅgāra* or *prema*. In aesthetics, *rati* elevated to the state of enjoyment is experienced as *śṛṅgāra-rasa*, "erotic" *rasa*. However, in bhakti yoga, the *sthāyi-bhāvas* are variations of *Kṛṣṇa-rati*, that is, different types of affection for Krishna. In this state of delight, the *sthāyi-bhāvas* are experienced as *bhakti-rasa*, "devotional *rasa*."

Moreover, although the components of *bhāva* in aesthetic *rasa* are the same as those in *bhakti-rasa*, they are understood in a different way: in the former, feelings are ordinary and come from the mind, while in the latter, emotions are of the soul and spirit: it is our authenticity emerging as emotion, it is feeling what we really are. In the end, *rasa* that inspires a play is ordinary because it is not related to *Kṛṣṇa-rati*, "loving affection toward God." Though *rasa* can be experienced through art, it is impossible to taste *bhakti-rasa* without *Kṛṣṇa-rati*.

Finally, to experience aesthetic *rasa*, spectators must have certain *vāsanās*, "subconscious mental impressions." But Rūpa Gosvāmī explains that devotional *rasa* arises from the divine aspect of bliss and love in our inner depths, from the very same essence of our existence. Moreover, what both the aesthetic and devotional *rasas* have in common is that they develop on the subject-object platform between the experiencer and what is experienced. That is to say, both happen in a dualistic setting, even though the veil between "I" and "That" is thin and subtle. This experience belongs to the first stages of bhakti yoga, in which devotees still perceive a difference between themselves and the Lord.

Components of *bhakti-rasa*

Sthāyi-bhāvas

The light of bhakti reveals a very rich world of devotional emotions, which make up the great treasures of bhakti yoga. The *bhāvas* gain spiritual value: from being simple emotions they become feelings awakened to the transcendental. From worldly emotions created by interactions between people and their surroundings, the *bhāvas* become human feelings for the beyond.

Love is the foundation of all aesthetic experiences; that is, *rati* is the basis of all the *rasas*. The other *bhāvas* are variations of love. When *rati* combines with components of *rasa*, it is expressed as different forms of love. *Sthāyi-bhāva* is our basic and permanent *rati*, "affection," toward God. The *ratis* are devotional *sthāyi-bhāvas*. They can be one of two types: principal or direct (*mukhya-ratis*), or secondary or indirect (*gauṇa-ratis*).

The *mukhya-ratis* – principal affections

The principal *ratis* are based on affectionate relationships with the Lord; they are divided into five classes that correspond to the five *vibhāvas* that cause them to manifest: *śuddha-rati*, *dāsya-rati*, *sakhya-rati*, *vātsalya-rati*, and *mādhurya-rati*.

1. *Śuddhā-rati*, "neutral, unqualified affection," is subdivided into *sāmānya* (general), *svaccha* (transparent), and *śānta* (peaceful).

   i. *Sāmānya-rati* is general affection that has not matured enough to express itself specifically to the Lord.
   ii. *Svaccha-rati* is a bhakta's affection that has not yet developed a focused devotion for the Lord and sometimes reflects different affections.
   iii. *Śānta-rati* is affection that blossoms in devotees who lean toward a passive relationship with the Lord.
2. *Dasya-rati* (also *prīti-rati*), "attentive affection": devotees experience their inferiority in the face of the immensity of the omnipotent Lord and feel dependent on divine mercy.
3. *Sakhya-rati*, "friendly affection": bhaktas feel equal with the Lord.
4. *Vātsalya-rati*, "parental affection": devotees feel superior to the Lord and instead of asking him for protection, want to protect him.
5. *Mādhurya-rati* (also *priya-rati*), "conjugal affection": the *gopīs* experienced this type of feeling for Krishna.

The *gauṇa-ratis*–secondary affections

The *gauṇa-ratis* are the seven remaining *sthāyi-bhāvas* in Bharata Muni's theory and are connected to *Kṛṣṇa-rati*. While the five *mukhya-ratis* are eternal, the seven *gauṇa-ratis* appear and disappear in different situations and leave strong impressions (*samskaras*) in the heart. Given these enduring impressions, *gauna-ratis* are classified as *sthāyi-bhāvas* and not *vyabhicāri-bhāvas*.

There are seven *gauṇa-ratis*:

1. *Hāsya-rati* (affectionate laughter).
2. *Vismaya-rati* (affectionate wonder).
3. *Utsāha-rati* (affectionate enthusiasm).
4. *Śoka-rati* (affectionate lamenting).
5. *Krodha-rati* (affectionate anger).
6. *Bhaya-rati* (affectionate fear).
7. *Jugupsā-rati* (affectionate disgust).

They are considered secondary emotions because they are not devotional, however, they transform into devotional emotions when they connect to one of the *mukhya-ratis*. For example, laughter is not related to affection for Krishna, but when a cowherd jokes with the Lord, the laughter connects to *sakhya-rati* (affectionate friendship) and thus reaches the level of spiritual affection and transforms into *hāsya-rati* (affectionate laughter). The *mukhya-rati* transmits its quality of *rati* to the *gauṇa* emotion, and thus transforms into *gauṇa-rati*.

Vibhāva

Vibhāva stimulates our affection for God so much that it elevates it to a great delight. It is divided into *ālambana*, "foundational," and *uddīpanas*, "stimulators." This is described in the following verse:

dvi-vidha 'vibhāva',— ālambana, uddīpana
vaṁśī-svarādi—'uddīpana', kṛṣṇādi—'ālambana'

> There are two classes of emotional stimulators. One is that which is called *foundational*, or *ālambana*, and the other awakening, or *uddīpana*. The vibration of Krishna's flute is an example of awakening, and Lord Krishna himself is an example of foundational *vibhāva*.
>
> (*Caitanya-caritāmṛta*, "*Madya-līlā*," 23.50)

Ālambana-vibhāva is itself subdivided into *viṣaya* (object) and *āśraya* (refuge). *Viṣaya* refers to the Lord, who is the object of devotion, and *āśraya* refers to the bhaktas, "devotees of the Lord," who constitute the refuge of all sincere aspirants.

Anubhāva

Anubhāva is a result of the intensification of the *sthāyi-bhāvas*. In the context of bhakti, this deals with an action that originates from the intensification of love for God, which in turn stimulates our love for him. *Anubhāva* is divided into two categories: *śita*, "weak," which does not involve intense physical movements of the body, and *kṣepaṇa*, "daring," which does.

The main examples of *śita* are singing in a low voice (*gīta*), yawning (*jṛmbhaṇa*), breathing heavily (*śvāsa-bhūmā*), leaving the presence of others (*lokānapekṣitā*), salivating (*lālāsrava*), groaning (*huṅkāra*), bleeding (*raktodgama*), and swelling of the limbs (*utphulla*). The main examples of *kṣepaṇa* are dancing (*nṛtya*), rolling on the floor (*viluṭhita*), stretching the body (*tanu-moṭana*), sobbing (*krośana*), laughing in a high voice like a lunatic (*aṭṭa-hāsa*), dizziness (*ghūrṇā*), and hiccupping (*hikkā*).

Vyabhicārī-bhāvas

Vyabhicārī-bhāvas are emotions that arise from *sthāyi-bhāvas*. For bhakti, this refers to emotional experiences that originate from a specific affection toward God, an experience that simultaneously intensifies this affection. There are thirty-three *vyabhicārī-bhāvas*: depression (*nirveda*), lethargy (*glāni*), suspicion (*śaṅkā*), jealousy (*asūyā*), intoxication (*mada*), fatigue (*śrama*), laziness (*ālasya*), misery (*dainya*), anxiety (*cintā*), fainting (*moha*), remembrance (*smṛti*), strength (*dhṛti*), shyness or embarrassment (*vrīḍā*), nervousness (*capalatā*), joy (*harṣa*), agitation or excitement (*āvega*), laziness (*jaḍatā*), pride or arrogance (*garva*), pain (*viṣāda*), discomfort (*autsukya*), sleepiness (*nidrā*), forgetfulness (*apasmāra*), drowsiness or being overcome by sleep (*supta*), waking (*vibodha*), intolerance (*amarṣa*), concealment (*avahitthā*), fury (*ugratā*), sickness (*vyādhi*), dementia (*unmade*), death (*maraṇa*), terror (*trāsa*), and argumentation or deliberation (*vitarka*).

Sāttvika-bhāva

Sāttvika-bhāva refers to an involuntary action that arises from love for the Lord that simultaneously increases it. The principal difference between *anubhāva* and *sāttvika-bhāva* is that the former emerges from lower states of consciousness influenced by *rajas* and tamas, while the latter is a reaction that comes from a sattvic heart overflowing with pure love for God. As mentioned previously, there are eight *sāttvika-bhāvas*: astonishment (*stambha*), perspiration (*sveda*), hair standing on end (*romāñca*), broken voice (*svara-bheda*), trembling (*vepathu*), paleness (*vaivarṇya*), tears (*aśru*), and fainting (*pralaya*).

Bhakti-rasa

According to *Gauḍīya* Vaishnavism, devotion for God is the only *rasa* that cannot come from the material plane. Krishna himself gives it to bhaktas. Human beings living in illusion want to find love in others, but this desire can only be truly satisfied in the Lord, who is *akhila-rasāmṛta-mūrti*, "the very manifestation of all sweetness," as stated in this verse:

akhila-rasāmṛta-mūrtiḥ prasṛmara-
ruci-ruddha-tārakā-pāliḥ
kalita-śyāmā-lalito
rādhā-preyān vidhur jayati

> Krishna, the destroyer of all suffering and the giver of all bliss, the very manifestation of all sweetness, surpasses all the others in glory. He subjugates Tārakā and Pālikā by spreading his beauty, he accepts Śyāmalā, Lalitā, and their peers, and gives pleasure to Rādhā through his excellent qualities.
>
> (*Bhakti-rasāmṛta-sindhu*, 1.1.1)

While previous authors limited themselves to the experience of *rasa* in the theatrical sphere, Rūpa Gosvāmī extended it to all of life because *rasa* is not a simple, temporary, aesthetic experience, but the culminating essence of a genuine human life.

Ordinary artists believe it is possible to experience

rasa by listening to poetry or seeing a play. However, according to Rūpa Gosvāmī, affection for Krishna (*Kṛṣṇa-rati*) is essential for the genuine experience of *rasa*. He explains that the trait of *bhakti-rasa* is *śuddha-sattva* (pure and luminous), unlike aesthetic *rasas* with natural attributes (sattva, *rajas*, tamas). Therefore, he maintains that there is only one true *rasa*: *bhakti-rasa*, which is the most elevated religious experience.

Bhakti-rasa is described in the following words:

vyatītya bhāvanā-vartma
yaś camat-kṛti-bhāra-bhūḥ
hṛdi sattvojjvale bāḍhaṁ
svadate sa raso mataḥ

> When one transcends the path of ecstatic love and is situated on the highest platform of pure goodness, it is understood that one has cleansed the heart of all material contamination. In this pure stage of life, one can taste the nectar, and the capacity to taste is technically called *rasa*, "transcendental sweetness."
>
> (*Bhakti-rasāmṛta-sindhu*, 2.5.132)

The transformation of bhakti into *bhakti-rasa* is produced by combining *rati* with certain *vibhāvas*, *anubhāvas*, *sāttvika-bhāvas*, and *vyabhicāri-bhāvas*, as this verse explains:

premādika sthāyi-bhāva sāmagrī-milane
kṛṣṇa-bhakti rasa-rūpe pāya pariṇāme
vibhāva, anubhāva, sāttvika, vyabhicārī
sthāyi-bhāva 'rasa' haya ei cāri mili'

When the permanent emotions [*sthāyi-bhāvas* such as neutrality, servitude, and so forth] mix with the other elements, love for God is transformed into transcendental sweetness. With the mixture of the stimuli (*vibhāva*), the reaction (*anubhāva*), the physical response (*sāttvika-bhāva*), and the transitory emotion (*vyabhicāri-bhāva*), the permanent emotional disposition (*sthāyi-bhāva*) is transformed into ever more delicious transcendental sweetness.
(*Caitanya-caritāmṛta*, "*Madhya-līlā*," 23.47–48)

Permanent and fundamental affection toward God is elevated to the point of tasting it, like devotional *rasa*. This growing love helps devotees break, one by one, the barriers that separate human nature from the Divine.

Mukhya-bhakti-rasas

Mukhya-bhakti-rasas are types of sweetness that correspond to the direct affections. These *rasas* are generated from the five *mukhya-ratis*: *śanta-bhakti-rasa*, *vātsalya-bhakti-rasa*, *sakhya-bhakti-rasa*, *dāsya-bhakti-rasa*, and *mādhurya-bhakti-rasa*. They all have their respective *vibhāvas*, *anubhāvas*, *sāttvika-bhāvas*, and *vyabhicāri-bhāvas*. Kṛṣṇadāsa Kavirāja Gosvāmi mentions them:

śānta, dāsya, sakhya, vātsalya, madhura-rasa nāma
kṛṣṇa-bhakti-rasa-madhye e pañca pradhāna

> There are five primary transcendental types of sweetness experienced with God: *śānta*, *dāsya*, *sakhya*, *vātsalya*, and *mādhurya-rāsa*.
> (*Caitanya-caritāmṛta*, "*Madhya-līlā*," 19.185)

Śānta-bhakti-rasa is peaceful and tranquil devotion toward the Lord. Devotees are only ready to develop *śānta-bhakti-rasa* after having developed indifference toward the desires of enjoyment and pleasure.

śamo man-niṣṭhatā buddher
dama indriya-saṁyamaḥ
titikṣā duḥkha-sammarṣo
jihvopastha-jayo dhṛtiḥ

> *Śama*, or *śānta-rasa*, indicates that one's mind is fixed on meditating constantly on me [the Lord]. *Dama* means controlling the senses and not deviating from the service of the Lord; *titikṣā* means tolerating unhappiness; *dhṛti* means completely controlling the tongue and genitals.
> (*Bhāgavata Purana*, 11.19.36)

Vātsalya-bhakti-rasa, "parental devotion": The corresponding *vibhāva* represents the first years of Krishna's incarnation, from infancy to five years of age. It is the compassion (*anugraha*) that an adult generally expresses for a child. Compassion for the Lord is the principal emotion of *vātsalya-bhakti-rasa.*

Sakhya-bhakti-rasa, "fraternal devotion": The corresponding *vibhāva* is the childhood of Krishna, between five and ten years of age.

Dāsya-bhakti-rasa, "affectionate devotion in service": The *vibhāva* is the late childhood and early adolescence of Krishna, between eleven and sixteen years of age. *Dāsya-bhakti-rasa* is a great affection, "*prīti*," for the Lord. Although all the *rasas* have *prīti*, servitude is called *prīti-rasa* because service is one of the first indications of affection toward the Lord.

tyayopabhukta-srag-gandha-
vāso-'laṅkāra-carcitāḥ
ucchiṣṭa-bhojino dāsās
tava māyāṁ jayema hi

> Simply by decorating ourselves with garlands, fragrant oils, clothing, and ornaments that you have enjoyed and eating the remnants of your food, we, your servants, surely conquer your illusory energy.
>
> (*Bhāgavata Purana*, 11.6.46)

Dāsya-bhakti-rasa is divided into *sambhrama-prīti*, "service with reverence and fear," and *gaurava-prīti*, "service with a respectful attitude": The servants of the Lord can be classified into four types: *adhikṛta-dāsas* are devas who have been empowered for certain service in the world, *āśrita-dāsas* are devotees who have found refuge in the protection of the Lord, *pāriṣada-dāsas* are ministers who offer personal service to the Lord, and *anuga-dāsas* are intimate followers of the Lord in the Indian cities Vraja and Dvārakā.

Mādhurya-bhakti-rasa, "conjugal devotion": The corresponding *vibhāva* is the youth of Krishna beginning at seventeen years of age. It is a secret topic that can be easily misinterpreted, so only more advanced bhaktas study it. Rūpa Gosvāmī mentions it briefly in his *Bhakti-rasāmṛita-sindhu* and later explains it in more detail in the *Ujjvala-nīlamaṇi*, which is a supplement for elevated devotees. *Mādhurya-bhakti-rasa* is the sweetest of all, which reaches a level of greater intimacy with Krishna.

Gauṇa-bhakti-rasas

The seven *gauṇa-bhakti-rasas* originate from indirect affections toward the Lord. They are mentioned in the *Caitanya-caritāmṛta*:

hāsya, adbhuta, vīra, karuṇā, raudra, bībhatsa, bhaya
pañca-vidha-bhakte gauṇa sapta-rasa haya

Moreover, of the five direct nectars, there are seven indirect nectars known as: humorous (*hāsya*), compassionate (*karuṇā*), angry (*raudra*), heroic (*vīra*), fearful (*bhaya*), disgusted (*bībhatsa*), and amazed (*adbhuta*).

(*Caitanya-caritāmṛta*, "*Madhya-līlā*," 19.187)

We reach *bhakti-rasa* only when we abandon personal dramas. Enlightenment does not happen within the walls of individual drama. If we remain closed within our own limited novel, we will not glimpse the story of reality. Bhaktas renounce their temporary story to live in the eternal dimension. Divine romance happens to them after they open themselves to the generic and impersonal.

Hence, bhakti is not simply one *rasa* among a great variety of feelings and emotions; it is devouring passion (*prema*) that fuses the aesthetic and the private in a totally new way centered on a privileged object of adoration. The *rasas* became a resource for the religious imagination to transform the world onto a stage where the soul is not a mere spectator, but the principal actor who acts for the satisfaction of a divine witness and begs for his intervention.

Art and religion

Rasa can be defined as an artistic or religious phenomenon—art has something religious and religion has something artistic. The topic of emotions touches on the delicate veil between art and religion, heart and soul, and sentimental and spiritual levels.

Art and religion are simultaneously similar and radically different. Their similarity resides in the fact that both transcend the material plane; their expressions on the physical plane are mere reflections. What they paint is not on the canvas; what they dance cannot be seen in their movements; what they say does not dwell in words; what they express cannot be heard in their songs. Both are expressed physically from distant planes. The voices of artists and religious people are heard in the museums and churches, however, both transmit from a distance. On the other hand, the difference between the two is the same as the difference between the mind and the soul.

Mozart is as distant from Śaṅkara as the mental realm is from the spiritual realm. Art can be very subtle and abstract, but still breathes in a mental atmosphere. Religion, on the other hand, belongs to the great beyond, the spiritual world, the soul.

Artistic and religious experiences demand renouncing the personal for the generic. Art and religion both touch the universal, but art becomes religion only when it rises above mental limits. Art is the expression of the artist's psychology in a piece of work; it becomes religious when it does not originate in the mind, but the soul. Art is born in the mind, religion in the beyond. Art may reach subtle and abstract levels, but is still mere art as long as it limits itself to manifesting the artist's subjectivity. Religion is art that emerges from a universal experience. As subtle as artists' creations may be, they originate in their own psychology; on the contrary, religious people transmit what blossoms in silence, from a void. Artists give us access to their past, but enlightened beings are doors to the present. Artists express themselves from yesterday, religious beings, from now. Artists manifest their misery; saints, their bliss. Artists create works of art while enlightened beings are their own magnum opus.

Art arises from a desire or need to express, while religious experience is in itself expressive. If artists are deprived of expressiveness, they feel frustrated. Artists are the principal rebels against restrictions on freedom of expression. On the contrary, enlightened beings are not slaves to desire or need because their expression is natural and spontaneous.

Art allows artists to empty themselves of their psychological complexes and to calm inner chaos. On the other hand, there are no conflicts that emanate from religious experience, which emerges from silence and peace. Existence itself is creative, as seen in trees, flowers, animals, and stars. Those in total harmony with life breathe with life and allow it to flow spontaneously through them.

When religion emanates from the mind, we call it *art*; when art comes from the soul, we call it *religion*. When identifying ourselves with what is physical, our feelings are instinctive. When identifying ourselves with our minds, our emotions are no longer expressed as barks but as songs. However, only by situating ourselves in the essence of what we are—in the soul—is religion born. From this great nothingness, divine art blossoms and that is religion.

CHAPTER 7

The Development of Devotees in *Saguṇa-Bhakti*

According to the scriptures, as devotees advance along the path of bhakti, their hearts become purified and hence their devotion intensifies. Rūpa Gosvāmī subdivides this process into three stages:

yaḥ kenāpy atibhāgyena
jāta-śraddho 'sya sevane
nātisakto na vairāgya-
bhāg asyām adhikāry asau

Adhikārīs, or those who are eligible for bhakti, are people who have the supreme fortune to be faithfully devoted to the Lord. They are not to be overly attached to the world, nor excessively detached from it.

(*Bhakti-rasāmṛta-sindhu*, 1.2.14)

uttamo madhyamaś ca
syāt kaniṣṭhaś ceti sa tridhā

Adhikārīs, "eligible devotees," may be classified into three levels: high, intermediate, and novice.
(*Bhakti-rasāmṛta-sindhu*, 1.2.16)

Kaniṣṭhādhikārīs, "novice devotees"

Novice devotees are called *kaniṣṭhādhikārīs*. The *Bhāgavata Purana* notes:

arcāyām eva haraye
pūjāṁ yaḥ śraddhayehate
na tad-bhakteṣu cānyeṣu
sa bhaktaḥ prākṛtaḥ smṛtaḥ

Prākṛta-bhaktas, "materialistic devotees," are at the lowest level. They faithfully worship the Lord in manifestations that can be worshipped, such as the deities in the temple, but do not worship the Lord manifested in his devotees.
(*Bhāgavata Purana*, 11.2.47)

Madhvācārya also describes these devotees, in the following way:

arcāyām eva saṁsthitam
viṣṇum jñātvā tad-anyatra
naiva jānāti yaḥ pumān
ātmano bhakti-darpataḥ

> Unable to perceive the omnipresence of Lord Vishnu, *kaniṣṭhādhikārīs* confine themselves solely to the temple. The ceremonial rituals they perform lead them to arrogance.
>
> (*Śrī Bhāgavata-tatpārya-nirnaya,* 11.2.47)

On this level, devotees' faith is weak and based on limited knowledge of the sacred scriptures. Their devotional motivations are external and superficial. They feel some attraction to religion, ceremonies, and deities, but not enough to establish a steadfast devotional life or fully accept a spiritual master. Their religious life and sadhana lack consistency and stability.

Kaniṣṭhādhikārīs do not often acknowledge saints and enlightened beings from other religious traditions and disapprove of any religion or spiritual wisdom other than their own. For this reason, they can easily offend other spiritual people due to their lack of discernment.

Novice candidates can be very dogmatic and even fanatic, believing that anyone who thinks differently or does not belong to their organization is condemned to hell. Many claim that only their religion is authentic; within their creed, only their path is true; and within their path, only their guru is genuine. This attitude can lead to considerable time spent in lengthy debates with those who have different beliefs with the goal of so-called of saving them.

Since they focus their attention mainly on the apparent and superficial, *kaniṣṭhādhikārīs* are easily impressed by organizations with many ashrams and temples or gurus who have numerous disciples and have written many books.

Madhyamādhikārīs, "intermediate devotees"

Candidates at this stage are called *madhyamādhikārīs*, who are described in this verse:

īśvare tad-adhīneṣu
bāliśeṣu dviṣatsu ca
prema-maitrī-kṛpopekṣā
yaḥ karoti sa madhyamaḥ

The second type of devotee is called *madhyama*, "intermediate." They offer their love to God and are sincere friends of every devotee of the Lord. They express compassion toward ignorant people who are innocent and avoid associating with those who are envious of the Lord.

(*Bhāgavata Purana*, 11.2.46)

In the *Hari-nāma-cintāmaṇi*, Bhaktivinoda Ṭhakur also describes this type of devotee with the following words:

kṛṣṇa-prema kṛṣṇa-bhakte maitrī-ācaraṇa
bāliśete kṛpā āra dveṣī-upekṣaṇa
karile madhyama-bhakta śuddha-bhakta hana
kṛṣṇa-nāmne adhikāra karena arjana

They feel love for Krishna, are friendly toward devotees, compassionate toward novices and the ignorant, and avoid associating with envious people. They are called *madhyama-bhaktas*, and [even at this stage] they are considered *śuddha-bhaktas*, "pure devotees." They are qualified to intone the holy name of Krishna."

(*Hari-nāma-cintāmaṇi*, 4.81-82)

Madhyamādhikārīs can be divided into three categories: *kaniṣṭha-madhyamas*, *madhyama-madhyamas*, and *uttama-madhyamas*.

Kaniṣṭha-madhyamādhikārīs, "novice-intermediate devotees"

Kaniṣṭha-madhyamādhikārīs possesses great faith but have limited knowledge of the sacred scriptures. They begin to comprehend that enlightened saints can belong to various religions and that different paths deserve equal respect because they lead to the same God.

Kaniṣṭha-madhyamādhikārīs place more emphasis on the teachings of their guru because their faith in the guru becomes stronger. Although their devotion is more elevated, it still stems from and remains largely based on external concerns.

These devotees have attained more steadiness and constancy in sadhana, but cannot yet become gurus, because despite following the master's teachings to the letter, they are incapable of also following them in spirit.

Madhyama-madhyamādhikārīs, "intermediate-intermediate devotees"

This is a very advanced stage in which candidates have dedicated their lives exclusively to the spiritual search. Ever deepening knowledge of the scriptures, these devotees are continuously engaged in remembering Krishna's pastimes or chanting the *mahā-mantra* with *rasa*, "taste." Their *anarthas*, "impurities," have almost disappeared and only vestiges remain. They are totally dedicated and no longer commit offenses of any kind. Although they are not fully realized, *madhyama-madhyamādhikārīs* can guide other devotees because they are connected to their guru's lineage.

Uttama-madhyamādhikārīs, "advanced-intermediate devotees"

These candidates have reached a state of self-realization and are fully capable of following the bhakti path. They have knowledge of the shastras and an unshakeable faith. They have totally surrendered themselves to their spiritual master, have realized who their guru really is, and live according to their guru's message.

Uttamādhikārīs, "the most elevated devotees"

The most elevated candidates are those who perform *uttama-bhakti*, which is service to God with a benevolent disposition of love, desiring only the Lord. Rūpa Gosvāmī describes it this way:

anyābhilāṣitā-śūnyaṁ jñāna-karmādy-anāvṛtam
ānukūlyena kṛṣṇānuśīlanaṁ bhkatir uttamā

Uttama-bhakti is service devoted to Krishna that is given freely and positively, without any desire for personal gain. It is unobstructed by intellectual knowledge (jnana) or fruitive actions (karma).
(*Bhakti-rasāmṛta-sindhu*, 1.1.11)

tadādi-pañca-saṁskāri
navejyā-karma-kārakaḥ
artha-pañcakavid vipro
mahā-bhāgavataḥ smṛtaḥ

Mahā-bhāgavatas, "great devotees of the Lord," have mastered the five practices of purification (*pañca-saṁskāras*) mentioned earlier. They are absorbed in the nine devotional activities (deity worship, mantra, yoga, *yajña*, prayer, *nāma-saṅkīrtana*, service, and worship of devotees and the Lord), and deeply understand the esoteric meaning of these activities.
(*Padma Purana* cited in *Bhakti-sandarbha*, 198.12)

The *Bhāgavata Purana* refers to *uttamādhikārīs* in the following way:

śrī-harir uvāca
sarva-bhūteṣu yaḥ paśyed
bhagavad-bhāvam ātmanaḥ

bhūtāni bhagavaty ātmany
eṣa bhāgavatottamaḥ

Sri Hari said: "The most advanced devotees (*uttama-bhāgavatas*) see God, the Self, in all things. Hence, they see everything in relation to the Lord, and understand that all that exists is eternally within God, the Self."

(*Bhāgavata Purana*, 11.2.45)

gṛhītvāpīndriyair arthān
yo na dveṣṭi na hṛṣyati
viṣṇor māyām idaṁ paśyan
sa vai bhāgavatottamaḥ

The greatest devotees (*uttama-bhāgavatas*) see the entire material world as Lord Vishnu's illusory potency (maya)—even while their senses continue to perceive objects—and hence feel neither attachment nor hatred for the things of this world.

(*Bhāgavata Purana*, 11.2.48)

na kāma-karma-bījānām
yasya cetasi sambhavaḥ
vāsudevaika-nilayaḥ
sa vai bhāgavatottamaḥ

Uttama-bhāgavatas (the most elevated devotees of the Lord) have taken sole refuge in Lord Vāsudeva. Their hearts are free of the seeds of karma and lust.

(*Bhāgavata Purana*, 11.2.50)

na yasya janma-karmabhyām
na varṇāśrama-jātibhiḥ
sajjate 'sminn ahaṁ-bhāvo
dehe vai sa hareḥ priyaḥ

Beloved devotees of the Lord are those who do not identify with their bodies, family lineages, pious activities, or exalted positions in the varnashrama; they humbly serve the Lord.

(*Bhāgavata Purana*, 11.2.51)

Uttamādhikārīs, also called *mahā-bhāgavatas*, "great devotees of the Lord," can descend to the *madhyamādhikārī* level to preach and accept disciples. In this way, they can adopt the role of *dīkṣā-guru* at the *madhyama* level to help others.

Uttama-bhaktas experience *rāga*, or an "intense passion," for the Lord similar to *rāgātmikā*, the "attachment" felt by residents of Vraja for Lord Krishna.

In the *Bhakti-rasāmṛta-sindhu*, *rāgātmikā-bhakti* is defined in this way:

iṣṭe svārasikī rāgaḥ
paramāviṣṭatā bhavet
tan-mayī yā bhaved bhaktiḥ
sātra rāgātmikoditā

Spontaneous love for a chosen deity must be completely captivating. This devotion is called *rāgātmikā-bhakti.*

(*Bhakti-rasāmṛta-sindhu*, 1.2.272)

Regarding *rāgātmikā-bhakti*, the following is noted in the *Caitanya-caritāmṛta*:

loka-dharma, veda-dharma, deha-dharma, karma
lajjā, dhairya, deha-sukha, ātma-sukha-marma
dustyaja ārya-patha, nija parijana
sva-jane karaye yata tāḍana-bhartsana
sarva-tyāga kari' kare kṛṣṇera bhajana
kṛṣṇa-sukha-hetu kare prema-sevana
ihāke kahiye kṛṣṇe dṛḍha anurāga
svaccha dhauta-vastre yaiche nāhi kona dāga
ataeva kāma-preme bahuta antara
kāma-andha-tamaḥ, prema-nirmala bhāskara
ataeva gopī-gaṇera nāhi kāma-gandha
kṛṣṇa-sukha lāgi mātra, kṛṣṇa se sambandha
ātma-sukha-duḥkhe gopīra nāhika vicāra
kṛṣṇa-sukha-hetuceṣṭa mano-vyavahāra
kṛṣṇa lagi' āra saba kare parityāga
kṛṣṇa-sukha-hetu kare śuddha anurāga

The *gopīs* have abandoned social customs, mandates of the scriptures, bodily requirements, fruitive actions, shyness, patience, bodily pleasures, self-satisfaction, and the varnashrama dharma path—which is difficult to abandon—as well as their own relatives and their relatives' punishments and rebukes, only to serve Lord Krishna. They offer their loving service solely for his satisfaction.

> This is called *firm attachment* to Lord Krishna. It is pure, like a clean unstained cloth.
>
> Lust and love are very different. Lust is like dense darkness, whereas love is like the spotless sun.
>
> There is not the slightest indication of lust in the *gopīs'* love. Their relationship with Krishna has no purpose other than Krishna's enjoyment.
>
> Their own pleasure or suffering has no importance for the *gopīs*. The ultimate aim of all their physical and mental activities is the enjoyment of Lord Krishna. They have renounced everything for the sake of Krishna. It is a pure attachment, in order to satisfy Krishna.
> (*Caitanya-caritāmṛta*, "*Ādi-līlā*," 4.167-172, 174-175)

Similarly, there are two classes of *rāgātmikā-bhakti*: *kāma-rūpā* and *sambandha-rūpā*, which are very clearly explained in the *Bhakti-rasāmṛta-sindhu*:

sā kāma-rūpā sambandha-
rūpā ceti bhaved dvidhā

> There are two different types of *rāgātmikā-bhakti*: *kāma-rūpā* is motivated by conjugal feelings, and *sambandha-rūpā* is motivated by the feelings of other types of relationships.
> (*Bhakti-rasāmṛta-sindhu*, 1.2.273)

For *uttamādhikārīs*, attachment to the Lord can be inspired by two kinds of feelings: *kāma-rūpā*, "conjugal," which is the romantic love for Lord Krishna experienced by the Vrindavana *gopīs*, and *sambandha-rūpā*, "from other types of relationships," which is the love for Krishna experienced by other residents of Vrindavana. *Uttamādhikārīs*' devotion is the highest of the dual platform of *saguṇa-bhakti*.

Chapter 8

The evolution of *saguṇa-bhakti*

In his *Bhakti-rasāmṛta-sindhu*, Rūpa Gosvāmī divides bhakti into three categories: sadhana bhakti (bhakti in practice), *bhāva-bhakti* (bhakti in ecstasy), and *prema-bhakti* (bhakti in pure love for God).

sā bhaktiḥ sādhanaṁ bhāvaḥ
premā ceti tridhoditā

There are three different types of bhakti: sadhana, *bhāva*, and *prema*.

(*Bhakti-rasāmṛta-sindhu*, 1.2.1)

Sadhana bhakti, "bhakti in practice"

Sadhana bhakti means engaging our minds and senses in the service of God, which leads to the manifestation of *bhāva-bhakti*.

Sadhana bhakti can be divided into two types: *vaidhī-bhakti* and *rāgānuga-bhakti*, as explained in the *Bhakti-rasāmṛta-sindhu*:

vaidhī rāgānugā ceti
sā dvidhā sādhanābhidhā

There are two types of sadhana bhakti: *vaidhī* and *rāgānugā.*

(*Bhakti-rasāmṛta-sindhu,* 1.2.5)

Vaidhī-bhakti is the ritualistic sadhana motivated by obedience to the guru or the shastras.

yatra rāgānavāptatvāt
pravṛttir upajāyate
śāsanenaiva śāstrasya
sā vaidhī bhaktir ucyate

Bhakti is called *vaidhī-bhakti* when actions flow from the teachings of the scriptures and not from the experience of *rāga* (intense attraction for the Lord).

(*Bhakti-rasāmṛta-sindhu,* 1.2.6)

In the same chapter, Rūpa Gosvāmī also notes:

śāstroktayā prabalayā
tat-tan-maryādayānvitā
vaidhī bhaktir iyaṁ kaiścin
maryādā-mārga ucyate

Vaidhī-bhakti, governed by the regulations of the sacred scriptures, is also called *maryādā* marga,

> "the path of laws or rules," by some [teachers such as Vallabhācārya]."
>
> (*Bhakti-rasāmṛta-sindhu*, 1.2.269)

On the subject of *vaidhī-bhakti*, the same scripture quotes the following verse from the *Nārada-pañca-rātra*:

surarṣe vihitā śāstre
harim uddiśya yā kriyā
saiva bhaktir iti proktā
tayā bhaktiḥ parā bhavet

> O Devarṣi, all activities prescribed in the scriptures related to the Lord are called *bhakti* [*vaidhī-bhakti*]. By performing them, one attains the most elevated [*prema*] bhakti.
>
> (*Bhakti-rasāmṛta-sindhu*, 1.2.13)

Rāgānuga-bhakti is the sadhana inspired by devotees who experience spontaneous attachment to God. They are eternal associates of the Lord known as *rāgātmikā-bhaktas*. Sooner or later, the nectar of *rāgātmikā-bhakti* will awaken in their hearts, because they closely follow the path of those who are intimately associated with Krishna.

rāgātmikā-bhakti-mukhyā vraja-vāsi-jane
tāra anugata bhaktira rāgānugā-nāme

> The inhabitants of Vrindavana, more than any others, are spontaneously attached to Krishna in

> *rāgātmikā-bhakti*. The devotion of those who follow in their footsteps is called *rāgānuga-bhakti*.
> (*Caitanya-caritāmṛta*, "*Madhya-līlā*," 22.108)

Devotion cannot be learned or taught like mathematics or geography. Love is not acquired by practicing a technique, nor is it the result of sadhana. Rather, it lies concealed and dormant in the depths of all beings. Therefore, it is important to understand the true place and value of spiritual practice.

Through sadhana, we create the necessary conditions for awakening devotion in our hearts and we prepare circumstances in which love manifests itself in all its glory.

Even a sentimental attachment between two human beings needs propitious circumstances. Couples seek romantic restaurants and places that offer favorable situations for enhancing emotional attraction. A young man is not likely to propose to his girlfriend in a smelly garbage dump. In the same way, as long as our mental activity contaminates us with envy, jealousy, resentment, material ambitions, and so on, the emergence of devotion will remain very doubtful. As long as the mind persists with its requirements and demands, trying to control and manipulate everything to meet its expectations, we will continue to confuse love with mundane emotional addiction.

The sadhana recommended by our spiritual master acts like a powerful purifier in devotees and liberates them from all impurities. Sadhana enables us to become vessels of grace, since God can be with us only to the extent that we are able to be with him.

Bhāva-bhakti, "bhakti in ecstasy"

The word *bhāva*, or spiritual "feeling or emotion" comes from the Sanskrit root *bhu*, which means "to be or to become." *Bhāva* is the state of ecstasy.

God is love, and being integral parts of God, love is the very essence of what we are. Although divine love, or *prema*, dwells in the depths of every being, in most people it remains in a latent state. According to Rūpa Gosvāmī, *bhāva* can reveal itself in the heart in two ways: through enthusiastic practice or through the compassion of the Lord or his devotees. In his *Bhakti-rasāmṛta-sindhu* (1.3.1), he cites the *Caitanya-caritāmṛta* to define *bhāva*:

śuddha-sattva-viśeṣātmā
prema-sūryāṁśu-sāmya-bhāk
rucibhiś citta-māsṛṇya-
kṛd asau bhāva ucyate

> When bhakti reaches the highest plane of pure *sattva*, it is like a ray from the sun of love. Devotion softens the heart by various emotional tastes. This state is called *bhāva*.
>
> (*Caitanya-caritāmṛta*, "*Madhya-līlā*," 23.5)

The essence of *bhāva* is *śuddha-sattva*, "pure sattva," which is the power of awakening our latent love and permitting us to feel emotions for God. Pure sattva is unlike worldly goodness (sattva), because it has not been mixed with *rajas* or tamas. When the *śuddha-sattva* power penetrates the heart of bhaktas through the grace of an enlightened spiritual master, *śuddha-sattva-viśeṣātmā*, "the distinguished plane of pure goodness," arises.

Śuddha-sattva is composed of *saṁvit-śakti* (cognitive power or granter of wisdom) and *hlādinī-śakti* (joyful or devotional power). The function of *saṁvit-śakti* is to bestow the capacity to perceive divinity, while that of *hlādinī-śakti* is to give bhaktas the bliss of divine love. Combining *saṁvit* and *hlādinī-śaktis* in the hearts of devotees awakens *bhāva-bhakti* and they taste ecstatic love.

The *Bhāgavata Purana* describes this process with exquisite beauty:

naṣṭa-prāyeṣv abhadreṣu
nityaṁ bhāgavata-sevayā
bhagavaty uttama-śloke
bhaktir bhavati naiṣṭhikī

> Through uninterrupted service to the saints, as well as the constant study of the scriptures, our evil inclinations are annihilated, and at the same time, a firm devotion to the Lord develops.
>
> (*Bhāgavata Purana*, 1.2.18)

tadā rajas-tamo-bhāvāḥ
kāma-lobhādayaś ca ye
ceta etair anāviddhaṁ
sthitaṁ sattve prasīdati

> The mind ceases to be affected by greed and lust, products of *rajas* and tamas, and becomes pacified in sattva.
>
> (*Bhāgavata Purana*, 1.2.19)

evaṁ prasanna-manaso
bhagavad-bhakti-yogataḥ
bhagavat-tattva-vijñānaṁ
mukta-saṅgasya jāyate

> In this way, direct realization of the Supreme Lord is manifested in those whose devotion to the Lord has led to serenity of mind and liberation from worldly attachments.
>
> (*Bhāgavata Purana*, 1.2.20)

bhidyate hṛdaya-granthiś
chidyante sarva-saṁśayāḥ
kṣīyante cāsya karmāṇi
dṛṣṭa evātmanīśvare

> When the Lord is revealed in the soul, the knots of the heart are loosened, doubts disappear, and accumulated karma and its fruits come to an end.
>
> (*Bhāgavata Purana*, 1.2.21)

Bhāva-bhakti appears when the bond that has existed eternally between a devotee and God is revealed.

Prema-bhakti, "bhakti in pure love for God"

The hint of light we see in the early morning is a sign that the sun will soon rise. If early morning light is like *bhāva*, *prema* is the sun itself—*bhāva* is the harbinger of *prema*. They are qualitatively the same but different in intensity of light and heat. The sun of love for God announces its presence by warming our heart through one of its rays, known as *bhāva*. In the *Caitanya-caritāmṛta*, we find the definition of *prema*:

samyaṅ-masṛṇita-svānto
mamatvātiśayāṅkitaḥ
bhāvaḥ sa eva sāndrātmā
budhaiḥ premā nigadyate

> Scholars give the name *prema* (pure divine love) to very intense *bhāva* that is endowed with a boundless feeling of being possessed by the Lord and which completely melts the heart.
>
> (*Caitanya-caritāmṛta*, "*Madhya-līlā*," 23.7)

The *Bhakti-rasāmṛta-sindhu* explains the origins of *prema-bhakti*:

bhāvottho 'ti-prasādotthaḥ
śrī-harer iti sa dvidhā

> There are two types of *prema* for the Lord: that which originates in *bhāva* and that which comes from the mercy of Sri Hari.
>
> (*Bhakti-rasāmṛta-sindhu*, 1.4.4)

It is not true that rituals are only for burgeoning disciples and not for enlightened masters. In the first stages, devotees participate in prescribed rites out of a sense of duty because they are recommended by sacred scriptures and gurus. However, rituals are not only for beginners: pure devotees, or great souls, continue to attend pujas, but only for the transcendental joy that they experience. Similarly, master acharyas who teach by example, continue inspiring disciples and followers by performing the limbs of bhakti.

It is not an easy task to please a millionaire with a gift. However, if we manage to please his child or his young grandson with a simple treat he will be very delighted. Similarly, pure devotees are beloved children of the Lord, and through them it is very easy to develop an intimate and direct relationship with him.

Prema-bhakti is not found in austerities or scriptures but in the heart of the Lord's devotees who have completely surrendered their lives to God. Only if we please pure devotees will Krishna be satisfied, and then *prema-bhakti* will be revealed in our heart. Viśvanātha Cakravartī Ṭhakur notes that there is only one way to attain *prema-bhakti*:

yasya prasādād bhagavat-prasādo
yasyāprasādān na gatiḥ kuto 'pi
dhyāyan stuvaṁs tasya yaśas tri-sandhyām
vande guroḥ śrī-caraṇāravindam

> By the grace of the spiritual master one attains the grace of the Lord. Without his grace, one cannot make any progress. Therefore, I must meditate and pray for the master's mercy three times a day and offer humble reverence to my spiritual master.
>
> (*Śrī-guru-devāṣṭaka*, 8)

So it is of paramount importance to be capable of recognizing true, pure devotees of the Lord and properly value the opportunity of being close to them.

The *Bhāgavata Purana* affirms this as well:

tulayāma lavenāpi
na svargaṁ nāpunar-bhavam
bhagavat-saṅgi-saṅgasya
martyānāṁ kim utāśiṣaḥ

> The value of even a moment's association with the Lord's devotees cannot be compared with anything, not even with the attainment of heaven or liberation from reincarnation, and much less so with the worldly blessings sought by mortal human beings.
>
> (*Bhāgavata Purana*, 1.18.13)

Any opportunity for association with an authentic bhakta must be made the most of, whether through studying, chanting, or simply being together in silence. However, all of this is nothing more than a pretext. The important thing is the association itself because although devotion cannot be given or taken, it can be acquired by infection. This is substantiated in this verse:

bhavāpavargo bhramato yadā bhavej
janasya tarhy acyuta sat-samāgamaḥ
sat-saṅgamo yarhi tadaiva sad-gatau
parāvareśe tvayi jāyate matiḥ

> When the material lives of wandering souls have ceased, O Acyuta, they may attain the association of saintly devotees. Only [this association] will awaken their devotion to you, since you are the true aim and the Lord of all causes and their effects.
> (*Bhāgavata Purana*, 10.51.53)

Since pure devotees bless others with their love for God, for the bhakta, they are nothing less than the divine grace of the Lord in human form. Simply finding ourselves in the presence of an elevated soul can liberate us from illusion, or maya. This is shown in the following verse:

sādhūnāṁ sama-cittānāṁ
sutarāṁ mat-kṛtātmanām
darśanān no bhaved bandhaḥ
puṁso 'kṣṇoḥ savitur yathā

> Merely being in the presence of a sadhu who has fully surrendered to me, eliminates material bondage just as the mere presence of the sun removes the darkness from one's eyes.
> (*Bhāgavata Purana*, 10.10.41)

For the bhakti yogi, association with pure realized devotees is essential and is one of the principal reasons to accept, serve, and live in the presence of a spiritual master. This is affirmed in this verse:

'sādhu-saṅga', 'sādhu-saṅga'
sarva-śāstre kaya
lava-mātra sādhu-saṅge
sarva-siddhi haya

The verdict of all revealed scriptures is that even a moment's association with a pure devotee brings with it the attainment of every success.
(*Caitanya-caritāmṛta*, "*Madhya-līlā*," 22.54)

The Lord bears the seed of wisdom and therefore he is the original spiritual master. Patañjali Maharishi confirms this:

tatra niratiśayaṁ sarva-jñatva-bījam

The seed of omniscience lies within him.
(*Yoga Sutra*, 1.25)

sa eṣaḥ pūrveṣām api guruḥ kālenānavacchedāt

God is the guru of the most ancient gurus; time does not limit him.
(*Yoga Sutra*, 1.26)

Mere intellectual knowledge can be acquired externally, but wisdom can only be born out of one's own depths. God dwells in our deepest core from whence the seed of wisdom springs, blossoming from and within consciousness. The true work of the master is not to inform disciples, but to stimulate their communion with the Lord, the original guru, the timeless and omniscient master. The experience of the Divine within us leads to the revelation that the spiritual master is the external manifestation of God.

Chapter 9

Parā-bhakti, "Transcendental Devotion"

In the early stages, bhakti is dualistic and called *saguṇa*, "with attributes." It consists of a triad (*tri-puṭī*) of lover, beloved, and devotion. This *saguṇa-bhakti* is conditioned by the three modes of nature and is only transcended upon reaching the heights of *nirguṇa-bhakti*, "bhakti without attributes," which is an Advaita Vedantic (non-dual philosophical) experience. It is called *parā-bhakti*, "transcendental devotion":

yasya deve parā-bhaktiḥ
yathā deve tathā gurau
tasyaite kathitā hy arthāḥ
prakāśante mahātmanaḥ

> Those who have transcendental love for the Lord and their spiritual master are truly great souls. Truths explained to these people reveal their own meanings.
>
> (*Śvetāśvatara Upanishad*, 6.23)

After purifying ourselves along various stages of *saguṇa-bhakti*, *parā-bhakti* will manifest and the mind will naturally flow toward the Divine. We see this confirmed in the following verse:

mad-guṇa-śruti-mātreṇa
mayi sarva-guhāśaye
mano-gatir avicchinnā
yathā gaṅgāmbhaso 'mbudhau

lakṣaṇaṁ bhakti-yogasya
nirguṇasya hy udāhṛtam
ahaituky avyavahitā
yā bhaktiḥ puruṣottame

Nirguṇa-bhakti manifests when, by the simple act of hearing about my [the Lord's] qualities, the mind flows naturally without motivation and without obstacles toward me, who dwells in the heart of everything, just as the waters of the Ganges River flow to the ocean.

(*Bhāgavata Purana*, 3.29.11-12)

sa eva bhakti-yogākhya
ātyantika udāhṛtaḥ
yenātivrajya tri-guṇaṁ
mad-bhāvāyopapadyate

As explained, this is essentially bhakti yoga, the highest platform by which one overcomes the

> three modes of nature (gunas) and reaches my [the Lord's] transcendental state.
>
> (*Bhāgavata Purana*, 3.29.14)

Worship arises from a supposed division between devotees and God, whereas in the experience of the omnipresent divinity, bhakti agrees with jnana: only God exists because his presence lies both within and without everyone and everything.

The spiritual paths differ, but they lead us to the edge of the same precipice, and the leap is one and the same for everyone: from the ego to the Whole, the personal to the universal, the relative to the transcendental. This is described in the following way:

> He gently oscillated back and forth across the dividing line. Ecstatic devotion to the Divine Mother alternated with serene absorption in the ocean of absolute unity. He thus bridged the gulf between the personal and the impersonal, the immanent and the transcendent aspect of reality.
>
> (*The Gospel of Sri Rāmakṛṣṇa*, "Introduction by Swami Nikhilānanda")

In the beginning, the paths taken by bhakti yoga and jnana yoga appear to be contradictory. However, when bhakti matures to the most elevated stages of *parā-bhakti*, the paths merge, like two rivers flowing into the same divine ocean of consciousness.

Both jnana and bhakti lead us to the realization of

our authentic nature, known as *sat-cit-ānanda*, "existence, knowledge, and absolute bliss." Bhakti's approach to the ultimate reality (*sat*) is through *ānanda* (eternal and absolute beatitude), while jnana's is *cit* (infinite transcendental consciousness). On the plane of the Absolute, there is no difference whatsoever between them, since they in fact constitute different aspects of the same reality. This is explained in the following way:

tvaṁ vā idaṁ sad-asad īśa bhavāṁs tato 'nyo
māyā yad ātma-para-buddhir iyaṁ hy apārthā
yad yasya janma nidhanaṁ sthitir īkṣaṇaṁ ca
tad vai tad eva vasukālavad aṣṭi-tarvoḥ

> O Lord! Certainly, you are this [world], both in its causal and manifested form. Yet you simultaneously keep yourself at a distance from it. Those in whom the universe's origin, manifestation, preservation, and dissolution coincide must necessarily be one with the universe. Just as the tree and its seed, or the crude earth and its subtle elements, you are present in all things as their substance, without being affected in the slightest by any change. For those who perceive this, any conflict between what is mine and others' is a senseless illusion.
>
> (*Bhāgavata Purana*, 7.9.31)

Parā-bhakti reveals to us that God lies both inside and outside of everything, and that in fact, nothing exists besides Krishna. This is affirmed in this verse:

oṁ īśāvāsyam idaṁ sarvaṁ
yat kiñ ca jagatyāṁ jagat
tena tyaktena bhuñjīthā
mā gṛdhaḥ kasya svid dhanam

> Here in this world, anything and everything that moves is pervaded and covered by the Lord. [Therefore,] only through renunciation are all things enjoyed. Do not covet the wealth of others.
> (*Śukla Yajur Veda*, 40.1.a and *Īśa Upanishad*, 1)

Jnana yoga provides an alternative explanation from the language of Advaita, "non-duality," which states that only the Self *is*:

brahma satyaṁ jagan mithyā
jīvo brahmaiva nāparaḥ
anena vedyaṁ sac-chāstram
iti vedānta-ḍiṇḍimaḥ

> Brahman (the Absolute) is real; this world is unreal and the individual soul is no different from Brahman. That by which this Truth is known is the truest science, the science of sciences. Thus proclaims Vedanta.
> (*Śaṅkarācārya*, *Brahma-jñānāvalī*, 18)

Jnana leads us to the experience that everything is illusion and that the only reality is the blessed Self. The final realization of the bhakta is that nothing exists besides God.

Jnani masters who have realized the omnipresent divinity define bhakti as the consciousness of our authentic nature. For example, Śaṅkarācārya refers to bhakti in this way:

mokṣa-kāraṇa-sāmagryām
bhaktir-eva garīyasī
sva-svarūpānusandhānam
bhaktir ity abhidhīyate
svātma-tattvānusandhānaṁ
bhaktir ity apare jaguḥ

> Of all the paths that lead to liberation, bhakti is supreme. Bhakti is the continuous contemplation of one's own essential nature. Others say that bhakti is the constant contemplation of one's own true nature.
> (*Viveka-cūḍāmaṇi*, 31-32a)

For Sri Ramaṇa Maharishi, the great jnani saint of Arunachala, "Bhakti is nothing more than to know oneself," as he once put it. Moreover, he went on to say that love is the experience of our essence. In his words: "The experience of the Self is only love, which is to see only love, to hear only love, to feel only love, to taste only love and to smell only love, which is bliss."

Due to a superficial understanding, some neo-Vedantists and novice devotees consider bhakti and jnana to conflict. Although bhakti yoga has been described as the simplest path, we should not underestimate its importance in our sadhana. Spiritual seekers who believe the way of devotion to be inferior will be unable to savor the nectarean ocean of *ānanda*. Even Śaṅkarācārya, the renowned advocate of Advaita Vedanta, was a great bhakta who worshipped deities and was dedicated to making pilgrimages to temples and sacred sites. He was also a brilliant composer of inspiring, devotional hymns. One of the most renowned hymns begins like this:

bhaja govindaṁ bhaja govindaṁ
govindaṁ bhaja mūḍha-mate
samprāpte san-nihite kāle
na hi na hi rakṣati ḍukṛñ karaṇe

> Worship Govinda, worship Govinda, worship Govinda, O deluded ones! It will not be laws and grammatical rules that will save you at the time of death.
>
> (*Bhaja-govindam*, 1)

In his commentary on the Bhagavad Gita (11.54), Śaṅkarācārya defines *ananyaya-bhakti*, "devotion without distraction," as "bhakti that never seeks any other object except the Lord, and by virtue of this, one does not recognize, through any of the senses, anything other than Vāsudeva."

In a process of diminution, devotees make themselves smaller before the greatness of Krishna; whereas jnanis embrace everything in an ever-expanding movement. The bhakta is like a little kitten who trusts its mother and surrenders to her care, while the jnani is like a baby monkey that must make the effort to embrace its mother.

In their first steps, bhaktas seek to relate to God, while jnanis aspire to be God. Bhaktas begin their path longing to taste God, while jnanis attempt to *become* That. Bhaktas aspire to relish the sweetness of honey, while jnanis yearn to become sweetness itself. However, the *Taittirīya Upanishad* tells us that consciousness itself is *rasa*.

yad vai tat sukṛtam raso vai saḥ
rasaṁ hy evāyaṁ labdhvā ''nandī bhavati
ko hy evānyāt kaḥ prāṇyāt
yad eṣa ākāśa ānando na syāt
eṣa hy evānandayāti

[The Absolute Truth] is in essence the divine taste (*rasa*). Attaining it, one becomes full of bliss. Who could live and breathe if this supreme space (*ākāśa*) of bliss did not exist? Essentially, this is what bestows bliss upon us.

(*Taittirīya Upanishad*, 2.7.2-3)

Lord Krishna refers to *jñānī-bhaktas* as the most elevated because they have experienced eternal unity with God, and consequently are no different from the Lord himself.

teṣāṁ jñānī nitya-yukta
eka-bhaktir viśiṣyate
priyo hi jñānino 'ty arthaṁ
ahaṁ sa ca mama priyaḥ

> Jnanis who are always engaged in constant, firm and [focused] bhakti stand out, because I love them and they love me.
>
> (Bhagavad Gita, 7.17)

In his commentary on this verse, Śaṅkarācārya says, that the bhakti of jnanis and meditation they experience are one, since they have become aware that there is nothing else to worship. He writes the following about verse 13.11:

> *"mayi cānanya-yogena bhaktir avyabhicāriṇī" mayi iti— mayi iśvare ananya-yogena— apṛthak-samadhinā "na anyo bhagavato vāsudevāt paraḥ asti, ataḥ sa eva naḥ gatiḥ" ity evam niścitā avyabhicāriṇī budhiḥ ananya-yogaḥ tena bhajanaṁ bhaktiḥ.*

> "Unwavering devotion to me by *ananya-yoga* (the yoga of non-deviation)." [Bhagavad Gita 13.11a]. [Commentary] *Mayi* [means] "to me, to the Lord." *Ananya-yogena* [means] "with no one or nothing else in mind." *Ananya-yoga* is a firm and resolute conviction that there is no other or higher being than Lord Vāsudeva and, therefore, he is our final refuge. Bhakti accompanied by this [firm conviction] is one of the means of wisdom.
>
> (*Śrimad Bhagavad Gita Bhāṣya* of Śrī Śaṅkarācārya on verse 13.11)

At its highest level, bhakti transcends religious structure. *Parā-bhaktas* renounce all effort and overcome any need for religious denomination or external symbols such as ceremonies, rituals, temples, and deities, though they are not necessarily abandoned. For them, there is no place that is not Vrindavana. The great sage of Pondicherry, Sri Aurobindo, explains this with these words:

> When external worship is interiorized, true bhakti begins. This deepens the intensity of divine love. This love leads to joy for the closeness of our relationship with the Divine; joy of closeness turns into the bliss of union.
>
> (*Synthesis of Yoga*)

Love is unity

Generally, people are considered religious if they believe in God and have faith in a supreme being. However, many of us have known so-called atheists who behave religiously and have observed religious people behaving like atheists.

Authentic religion does not reside in faith or in a belief in God, but in love. The mandate of my religion is not that we believe in God first and then we love. Rather, it is the reverse because our only chance to know God is by loving. Hence, authentically religious people are unmistakable, not for their attire but for their capacity to love. Although it is said that God is love, in reality, love is God; ultimately, religious beings are those who love.

Love is the unity that lies at the base of creation, and it is the very essence of consciousness, of Brahman. Those who love are associating with the Lord; the more intense one's love is, the more intimate is one's closeness to God. Krishna says:

bhaktyā tv anayayā śakya
aham evaṁ-vidho 'rjuna
jñātuṁ draṣṭuṁ ca tattvena
praveṣṭuṁ ca parantapa

> O Arjuna, destroyer of enemies! Only through total devotion is it possible to see me in this real form, know me, and penetrate me.
>
> (Bhagavad Gita, 11.54)

If bhaktas are unable to renounce their ideas, concepts, and conclusions about love, their devotion will be no more than mental phenomena. But if they manage to transcend the mind on the path of the heart, bhakti will manifest itself as their own presence, in all its purity and splendor.

When devotees awaken to the reality that nothing exists outside of God, they realize that just as Krishna resides in everyone and everything, his true essence dwells within devotees. With this realization, the phenomenon of the ego disappears and only God remains.

Only by forgetting what is private is the manifestation of the universal permitted, as the Whole declines to express itself in the particular. Ego is a social phenomenon that belongs to the masses; love flourishes in the individual. Ego is false; love is genuine. Ego is fearfulness; love is brave. Ego tries to possess; love allows itself to be possessed. Ego is illusory; love is real. Hence, the presence of the Divine only manifests itself when we forget ourselves as personal phenomena.

We disappear to the extent that we love, because our small "I" ceases to be the most important thing. Our lives stop egoistically revolving around ourselves and others become the center of our attention. Love teaches us that our own benefits and interests are insignificant; instead, we are thrilled by the happiness of others and saddened by their pain. Gottfried Leibniz (1646-1716) said that to love is to make the happiness of others your own happiness.

Just as cold dissipates in the presence of heat and darkness fades in the presence of the light, the ego cannot remain in the presence of love. They are incompatible. Love is like a powerful acid that dissolves the illusion of ego and evaporates all the beliefs that we harbor about ourselves. Love means renouncing that artificial center called "*I*." As the renowned Swiss philosopher and moralist Henri Frederic Amiel (1821-1881) once stated: "Love is the forgetfulness of the 'I'."

Love that flows toward the individual is a type of idolatry, but those who have opened their eyes to consciousness experience *akṛtrima-bhakti* (natural, authentic devotion), *sahaja-bhakti* (spontaneous, innate devotion), or *advaita-bhakti* (non-dual devotion). They stop being attracted by others' qualities and love the divinity that resides within. Bhaktas are no longer seduced by what others possess, but are attracted to what they really are.

Those who are awakened dwell in divine omnipresence. They know that love for anything in particular is because the universal is found within it. The sage Yājñavalkya states the following when instructing his wife Maitreyī:

ātmanas tu kāmāya sarvaṁ priyaṁ bhavati

It is for the Self that all is loved.
(*Bṛhad-āraṇyaka Upanishad*, 2.4.5)

Since only God is, we cannot love anything that is not the Divine. Though our love may be physical, emotional, or mental, it is always directed to God. When we realize his omnipresence, our limitations disappear and we recognize that God is sole cause of love.

Nevertheless, the duality of the lover and the beloved is necessary at first because it is unlikely that love will arise if it is not directed toward someone. If this separation between lovers is maintained, their love eventually cools and gradually disappears. In contrast, if the lovers draw nearer and nearer until, finally, there is no separation between them, the fire of their love will intensify and melt all boundaries.

Like in the early stages of a romance, devotees perceive the Lord to be separate from them. However, with the realization of divine omnipresence, love ceases to be the experience of a subject relating to an object.

Since the lover and beloved are interdependent, any division between them vanishes when duality is transcended. Then, as the experience of bhakti heightens, all barriers disappear: even though Īśvara and the bhakta seem to be superficially separated, they have become one in essence.

The path of bhakti begins as a romance, hearing and speaking about the beloved. Then there are emotions, closeness, and attachment, until a relationship is established. Then a deep thankfulness blooms from the greatest intimacy, which can only be expressed in prayer. But it is not a verbal prayer, a series of words expressed out of need, fear, or greed. Devotion transforms us into a prayer of joy, happiness, bliss, and ecstasy, which is expressed throughout our being. Our movements, our glances, and our steps are transformed into the worship of life, existence, and God.

So cease to be someone: you will not be a devotee who prays. Instead, all that remains will be the presence of a silent ecstatic prayer of gratitude. Worship ignites the fire of love and its heat melts the ego. Then, as the flame of divine passion intensifies, you will evaporate as a devotee and only purity will remain. Whatever began will return to ashes. The eternal will remain, overflowing with blessings.

In this nothingness, the sacred Self reveals itself to itself as absolute bliss. Only emptiness allows for subjective devotion of the Self, for the Self, in, from, and beyond the Self.

Chapter 10

Religion

As we look around, we see a world in a state of constant transformation. It is difficult for us to accept that life is fleeting and ephemeral, although we are aware that our body passes from childhood to adulthood and we know that old age will arrive, and finally, death.

Life is insecurity: at some point, we may attain everything we have desired, and in the next moment, we may lose it all. The present is unpredictable, anything can happen, and anything is possible: health and illness, strength and weakness, attachment and hatred, wealth and poverty, honor and humiliation. Like a constantly spinning wheel, life lifts us up at times and casts us down at others; today we can be at the top and tomorrow we may hit rock bottom.

Insecurity is the essence of life, just as heat is the essence of fire and wetness is the essence of water. Therefore, our attitude toward insecurity will determine our relationship with life. Our fear of existence's instability is one of the main forces that impels us to act.

However, chasing after a sense of security, we flee from life and thus do not perceive what is vital. Security is a type of death because only in a cemetery's tombs does nothing unexpected happen. Fear of uncertainty deprives us of life.

Human beings stray from the path to bliss when they give in to the temptation to feel secure and when they console themselves with temporary psychological relief. The problem lies in striving to reach a *feeling* of security that is merely an illusion. For example, if we fear loneliness, we may get married for the sense of companionship. However, just as feeling like a great artist does not make you a talented painter and acting like a millionaire does not improve your economic situation, having a partner, children, and grandchildren will not guarantee lifelong companionship. Thus, instead of living in the real world of facts, we move in a theoretical realm of ideas, feelings, and emotions.

Moreover, if we manage to find some sense of psychological security in money, our own home, the latest car, or a family, we will be faced with routine and boredom. We may feel safe, but deadened by and disconnected from life. Since illusory security is incompatible with the experience of reality, our efforts to feel secure will interfere with our inquiries and prevent us from exploring life.

Nevertheless, people continue to pursue this feeling of security by adopting certain ideals, such as nationalism, capitalism, etc. Eventually, recognizing that the world cannot offer them security, some even seek refuge in religion. With promises of a comfortable life in paradise, religions tempt those ready to adopt any doctrine—however absurd or senseless—to calm their own fears.

It is not the beliefs themselves that are important, but the relief that they offer to those seeking psychological security in this way.

Unfortunately, those who take refuge in a belief system can become very violent. One only has to look at all the wars, acts of torture, and crimes that have been committed throughout history in the name of religion. When questioned, such believers tend to react aggressively with the aim of defending the sense of security they have attained through their religious dogma. Fanaticism is not only the disease of religion, but it is also the greatest hazard of bhakti yoga.

The term "religion" generally denotes a belief system with a creed, theology, institutions, symbols, rituals, traditions, and clergy. Anyone who professes a specific "ism" is usually considered religious. However, not every faithful believer—whether Jewish, Christian, Muslim, or Hindu—seeks something real. Not everyone who attends a mosque, temple, synagogue, or church every Friday, Saturday, or Sunday is truly interested in a direct experience of God, nor does every member of a religious organization sincerely aspire to the Truth. In the absence of questioning and inquiring, merely being part of an organization will not radically change the lives of its members.

If we do not understand religion and use it incorrectly, it can become a serious hindrance in our spiritual lives. Our beliefs and traditions may hide the fact that we have utterly abandoned our search for the Truth and the fact that we consider ourselves to be believers may disguise our lack of devotion. In this way, despite believing we are religious, we may be mere *religionists* who, instead of seeking God, try to flee from him.

Faith can be either a help or a hindrance on the path toward God. Religion conditions us when it becomes restrictive, preventing us from sincerely questioning or investigating. In such cases, we end up blindly accepting a creed, settling for a feeling of relief and consolation. On the other hand, faith can help us if it is accompanied by the art of searching and a truly religious spirit.

The spiritual search

Any search impelled by the need for security will be reduced to a simple attempt to find consolation. And, since what we are searching for has already been registered in our memory, this process leads us to project our past and avoid the present. Such a search can never lead us to a discovery of any kind, but only to the identification of what we had expected to find.

But not everyone looks for security. There are those who perceive the ever-changing world and begin to question its existence. The temporary nature of life prompts them to ask whether something permanent exists beyond this fluctuating world of ups and downs, happiness, sorrow, laughter, and tears. Blessed are the brave who are bewildered by life, because the aspiration to inquire will arise within them!

Those who accept uncertainty and surrender completely to the unknown will embrace life. Their spiritual quest will lead them to the true revelation of the mystery.

Although the divine seed lies deep within each and every one of us, it will not germinate if it is not fertilized by an aspiration for the Truth. The desire for authenticity is the determining factor in its revelation.

The greater the intensity of our thirst, the greater the possibility that the Truth will be revealed within us. While few experience God, fewer still are blessed with a sincere longing for him. For that reason, bhakti yogis yearn more to desire the Truth than experience it. They believe that genuine grace is not the experience of God, but the longing for him from the depths of the heart.

tad viddhi praṇipātena
paripraśnena sevayā
upadekṣyanti te jñānaṁ
jñāninas tattva-darśinaḥ

> Know that by approaching those who know through humble exploration and service, those who have seen Truth will teach you the wisdom.
> (Bhagavad Gita, 4.34)

Here the Gita is referring to two key duties of disciples: to serve and explore. This means that discipleship is not just serving but also questioning and investigating. A true disciple is a religious person who lives in a constant search for the Truth.

The ordinary student has questions and invests energy in finding a guru who will respond to them. However, authentic spiritual devotees question even their own doubts.

They develop as disciples when they begin sincerely investigating. As soon as they are ready, their master will appear. They will recognize their master without being able to know if he or she is trustworthy because only one enlightened being can recognize another, just as only a physician can identify a good doctor.

The man of religion is a tireless seeker, an investigator, a researcher, a scientist of the subjective, and therefore, an attentive being. The true initiation of spiritual life is marked by an exploration of the real beyond the ephemeral. Inquiry is the call to meditation.

The logic of the mind states that before we can love something, it is necessary to know it. But the heart knows that only by loving can we truly know.

If we study botany, we will gather information about flowers. But only if we love them, will we come to know the essence of a lily or a rose. If we obtain a degree in zoology, we will acquire knowledge about animals, but only by loving them will we appreciate the nature of a dog or cat.

The mail carrier knows our address, the grocer our name, and the mechanic our car. However, only one who loves us, really knows us, understands our gestures, identifies our moods, and perceives our presence, perfume, and energy. Similarly, though some may settle for knowing God's supposed "name and address," those who wish to know him deeply must cultivate true bhakti.

According to bhakti yoga, ignorance is not a lack of information but an inability to love because we know only as much as we love. Bhakti yogis understand that someone who acquires extensive knowledge will merely become a learned person; sages will only be revealed as those who love. As they investigate, their findings begin transforming into love. So bhakti yogis are not religious scholars, but lovers of life and existence. In that love, they find God.

On this, we have the following words of the great master Sri Ramakrishna:

> M.: "When one sees God, does one see him with these eyes?"
>
> Sri Ramakrishna: "God cannot be seen with these physical eyes. In the course of spiritual discipline, one gets a 'love body,' endowed with 'love eyes,' 'love ears,' and so on. One sees God with those 'love eyes.' One hears the voice of God with those 'love ears.' One even gets a sexual organ made of love."
>
> With these words, Mr. M. burst out laughing. The master continued unperturbed: "With this 'love body' the soul communes with God."
>
> M. again became serious.
>
> Sri Ramakrishna: "But this is not possible without intense love of God. One sees nothing but God everywhere when one loves him with great intensity. It is like a person with jaundice who sees

> everything yellow. Then one feels, 'I am verily he.' A drunkard, deeply intoxicated, says, 'Verily I am Kali!' The *gopīs*, intoxicated with love, exclaimed, 'Verily I am Krishna!' One who thinks of God, day and night, beholds him everywhere. It is like a man seeing flames on all sides after he has gazed fixedly at one flame for some time."

The religion of bhakti yoga

Faith is a key that can open or close doors, and thus it can either help us to transcend ignorance or imprison us in the blindness of fanaticism. According to the way it is used, a belief system can lead to freedom or to conditioning. In this sense, the guidance of a genuine spiritual teacher becomes essential in learning to work properly with religious doctrines.

śrī-yadur uvāca
kuto buddhir iyaṁ brahmann
akartuḥ su-viśāradā
yām āsādya bhavāl lokaṁ
vidvāṁś carati bāla-vat

> Sri Yadu said: "O *brāhmaṇa*, you are not engaged in any religious practice, so from where have you acquired this great wisdom by which you travel freely throughout the world behaving as if you were a child?"
>
> (*Bhāgavata Purana*, 11.7.26)

Bhakti yoga is a path strongly linked to the religious phenomenon, though not necessarily to religions. As society socializes religions, it distorts and contaminates them with politics, divesting them of all spirituality.

The religious institution, as a physical entity, can be very helpful when it provides a framework for spiritual development. Because society requires certain order, there is no problem in establishing a religious institution, giving it a name, and dedicating a building to its members. However, the physical aspect of religion will only benefit its followers if it serves as no more than a means to facilitate their evolution. The true difficulty arises when the religious organization ceases to be a means and becomes an end in itself. As its members view life and the world through the distorted prism of their religious group, psychological institutionalization leads them to ignorance and bigotry.

For this reason, bhakti yoga accepts the establishment of religious institutions, as long as religion does not become internally institutionalized in the hearts of followers.

Truly religious people do not cultivate religious egoism or insist on any type of spiritual monopoly. Nor do they proclaim to be God's chosen one or the sole possessor of the Truth; this can only lead to offenses, hatred, persecution, resentment, division, war, and bloodshed in the name of religion. Bhakti yogis should avoid the dangerous spiritual aberration of fanaticism by shunning derogatory or offensive attitudes toward other devotional paths that are based on different theologies and liturgies.

The *Sanātana-dharma* religion remains open to all wisdom, regardless of the saint or religion it stems from:

ā no bhadrāḥ kratavo yantu viśvataḥ

May auspicious inspiration come to us from every direction.

(*Rig Veda*, 1.89.a)

prāmāṇya-buddhir vedeṣu
sādhanānām-anekata
upāsyānām-aniyamaḥ
etad dharmasya lakṣaṇam

The Vedas are regarded as the books of evidence. There are many different methods of worship (sadhanas). There is no fixed [binding] rule for the objects of worship. These are the characteristics of dharma.

(Sri Lokamānya Tilak)

Hinduism is nonsectarian; the holy scriptures are not directed at one particular group of human beings, but to all people in all times and places. The sacred Veda is broad enough to offer a shared sanctuary for any authentic religious experience:

anantā vai vedāḥ

The Vedas are indeed infinite.

(*Taittirīya Brāhmaṇa*, 3.10.46)

While most religions are based on a book, the foundations of *Sanātana-dharma* are not based on written scriptures. They are based on the transcendental experiences of the Vedic rishis, a fact that clearly underscores their individual nature. *Sanātana-dharma* is also called *Viśva-dharma*, which means "universal religion," because it treats saints of different spiritual paths as equally authentic. It acknowledges that they have arrived at the same Truth, though each has tried to transmit it according to one's own individuality, adapting it to the era, language, and culture.

Religious people are not conditioned by a system of beliefs but use religion as a means to liberation from conditioning. In this way, bhakti yogis consciously adopt a creed as a tool to access the mystery.

The person of religion

Unfortunately, the vast majority of humans suffer from sleepwalking. Both their beliefs and atheism are projected from their dreams. Any "ism" that transpires in our dream world merely provides us with comfort and tranquility to continue sleeping. In contrast, true religion awakens us.

Our experiences in the waking state are nothing more than mental projections. What we call *reality* is simply an extended dream that happens with our eyes open, but it is not essentially different from our dream experience. Instead of observing, we project the known onto the observed and end up dreaming while awake.

On this subject, there is a beautiful Hindu story I heard from my master. An elderly man lay sound asleep on the side of the street. The locals and neighborhood folk called him *sleepyhead* because he had been sleeping for more than fifty years. Everyone wondered what might have caused such an extended slumber, but they could find no answer. It was the eldest of the townspeople who one day said: "Gentlemen! I know why 'sleepyhead' has not awakened. It is simply because as he sleeps, he dreams that he is awake."

Human beings dream of themselves awake; they are what they dream of being. Bhakti yogis are religious beings but do not follow a God projected from their dreams. Rather, they surrender to the living God.

Bhakti yogis are, above all, beings of watchfulness, because attention always accompanies love. To the degree that we love, our attention arises spontaneously without any effort on our part. Love awakens us to life because the more aware we are, the more alive we are. Love leads us to life, which is God.

Our lack of observation makes us sleepwalkers and impels us to live irreligiously. In contrast, authentic bhakti yogis are beings of awareness, because remaining attentive and meditative are essential qualities for accessing reality.

Awareness means observing what is as it is, without interpretation or projecting our ideas, concepts, and conclusions on what we observe. The closer our attention, the subtler the phenomena we can observe.

Scriptures, beliefs, and ceremonies create the essential conditions, but ultimately, no one and nothing external can help us develop greater awareness. A spiritual master can only open our eyes with the torch of wisdom but he cannot see for us. Observation can only be learned from and within oneself.

Our first steps on the path of bhakti will be accompanied by the notion of a God who created the world, who is separate from us and lives in paradise. As long as we perceive our existence as an objective reality within time and space, we will surely relate to a personal God. However, at higher stages, we awaken to the reality that God is not someone or something, but everyone and everything. God does not exist, but is existence itself, and existence is God. God is the Absolute Truth. He is life. He is the only thing that really is.

Glossary of Sanskrit terms

A

***Ācāra*:** Behaviour, conduct.

Acharya: A highly respected Hindu teacher who has mastered a topic, specifically a guru or spiritual master who instructs on the Vedas, laws of sacrifice, and religious mysteries. In Vaishnava terminology, the title is used to denote a spiritual master who teaches by example and sets the appropriate religious example for all human beings.

Advaita: "Not two," a synonym for "non-duality." This is the experience that there is no separation between subject and object, between the "I" and the Whole.

Ahankara: Ego.

***Alaṅkāra*:** Ornaments in traditional Sanskrit rhetoric, specifically an ornament of sense or sound.

***Ānanda*:** Absolute transcendental happiness, bliss.

***Aṅgas*:** Limbs.

***Ānukūlyasya saṅkalpa*:** A resolution for something favorable for the development of devotion to God.

***Arcana*:** Worship.

Ashram: A hermitage or spiritual community.

Atma: The Self.

***Ātma-nivedana*:** Complete surrender to the Divine.

***Ātmā-sākṣātkāra*:** Realization of the Self.

***Ātma-śakti*:** The power of the Self.

***Avadhūta*:** A highly spiritually developed soul, a great soul.

***Avidya*:** Ignorance.

B

***Bali*:** Offering.

Bhagavad Gita: "The Song of God," the most essential and widely accepted text by all *Sanātana-dharma* philosophies and paths. It is a conversation between Lord Krishna and his disciple Arjuna in the battlefield of Kurukṣetra, in which Krishna explains the essence of spiritual practice and knowledge.

Bhagavān: Personal aspect of God.

***Bhāgavata Purana*:** Also called *Śrīmad Bhāgavatam*. A scripture of 18,000 verses compiled by the sage Vyāsa; the most famous, beautiful, and poetic of the eighteen great Puranas.

***Bhajana*:** Adoration, also used to describe the intonation of songs of worship for the Divine.

Bhakta: A devotee.

Bhakti: Devotion, love.

Bhakti yoga: The yoga of devotion. A process of union with the Divine through the development of love for God through worship.

***Bhāva*:** Literally, "transform, to be, or a form of being."

It is often used to denote a mood, emotion, or feeling.

***Bhoga*:** Materialism, enjoyment and pleasure.

Brahman: The Supreme and Absolute Consciousness.

C

***Caitanya-caritāmṛta*:** Biography of Sri Caitanya, written by Kṛṣṇadās Kavirāj Gosvāmī.

***Chāndogya Upanishad*:** One of the ten oldest and most authoritative Upanishads.

D

***Darśana*:** Literally, "vision."

***Dāsya*:** Service with a devotional attitude.

Devarṣi Nārada: Heavenly rishi. One of the greatest devotees of the Lord Vishnu.

Devas: Gods.

Devi: Divine Mother.

Dharma: Law, religion, duty, morals, or literally, "that which is established."

Dhyana: Meditation. The seventh stage of *aṣṭāṅga-yoga*.

***Dīkṣā*:** Initiation.

***Divya*:** Divine.

***Divya-deva-sevana*:** Service to the Divine.

G

Gaṇeśa: God with the head of an elephant, the remover of obstacles.

Garga Muni: Spiritual master of Lord Krishna.

***Gopīs*:** Young milkmaids in Vrindavana, India. The divine lovers of Sri Krishna.

***Gosvāmī*:** Master of the senses. One who has complete control over one's senses. It is also used as an honorary title.

Guna: One of the three qualities or modes of nature.

Guru: Literally, "big or heavy." A master and spiritual guide in Hinduism.

I

***Iṣṭa-devatā*:** A form of God chosen individually for one's main worship and devotion.

Īśvara: Supreme Controller.

***Īśvara-praṇidhāna*:** Surrender to God.

J

***Japa*:** Repetition of holy names or mantras while holding prayer beads.

Jnana: Knowledge.

Jnana yoga: The yoga of knowledge.

K

Karma: Action.

Karma yoga: The yoga of action.

***Kīrtana*:** Chanting the names and the glories of the Lord.

Krishna: One of the avatars of Lord Vishnu.

M

***Mādhyamā*:** Intermediate.

***Mahābhārata*:** A great epic that narrates a royal conflict that leads to a great war. It includes the Bhagavad Gita. It was composed by Śrīla Vyāsadeva, and is sometimes known as the fifth Veda.

***Mahā-mantra*:** The great mantra—*Hare Kṛṣṇa Hare Kṛṣṇa Kṛṣṇa Kṛṣṇa Hare Hare Hare Rāma Hare Rāma Rāma Rāma Hare Hare.*

***Maṅgala-ārati*:** Morning deity worship.

***Maṅgalācaraṇa*:** Auspicious invocation.

Mantra: A sacred phrase or mystical, sacred word.

Maya: The power of illusion.

Moksha: Liberation.

***Mṛdaṅga*:** A double-headed drum used in southern India's classical music.

P

***Pāda-sevana*:** Rendering service to the feet of the Divine or to the guru.

***Paramparā*:** Guru-disciple lineage.

Patañjali Maharishi: The compiler of the *Yoga Sutra*.

***Prema*:** Divine love.

Puranas: Hindu scriptures that reveal the Vedic message and its values in a simple way, mainly through traditional stories about saints, kings, and great devotees.

Purusha: The Supreme Being or internal spirit.

R

***Rāga*:** Attraction or mood, generally used to describe melodic moods in Indian classical music.

***Rajo-guṇa* or *rajas*:** The material mode of passion, one of the three gunas, "the modes of nature."

***Rig Veda*:** One of the four Vedas.

Rishi: A seer, a self-realized sage.

S

Sadhana: Spiritual practice.

***Sādhu-saṅga*:** Association with holy people.

***Sakhya*:** Friendship.

Shakti: Power.

Samadhi: Complete union with the Divine. The last of the eight stages of ashtanga yoga.

***Sanātana-dharma*:** Literally, "eternal religion," or Hinduism.

Śaṅkarācārya: The main advocate of the Advaita Vedanta school of philosophy.

***Saṅkīrtana*:** Chanting and glorifying God.

***Śaraṇāgāti*:** Literally, "taking refuge." Surrendering to the Lord.

Shastra: Scripture.

Satsang: Associating with the Truth.

***Sattva-guṇa* or sattva:** Material mode of goodness and clarity.

***Sevā*:** service.

Shloka: Verse.

***Śravaṇa*:** Listening, hearing.

***Śrīmad Bhāgavatam*:** See *Bhāgavata Purana*.

***Śuddha-bhakti*:** Pure devotion.

***Svādhyāya*:** Study of scriptures, one of the *niyamas*.

Swami: One who has accepted the renounced order of life.

T

***Tamo-guṇa* or tamas:** The material mode of darkness or ignorance. One of the three gunas.

V

***Vaidika-dharma*:** Vedic religion, Hinduism.

***Vaikuṇṭha-loka*:** A realm in the spiritual world. The dwelling of Lord Nārāyaṇa.

Vaishnavism: A path within the Hindu religion that focuses on worshipping Lord Vishnu, the sustainer in the Trinity.

Vedanta: Literally, "the finalization of the Vedas." The final conclusion and the essence of the Vedas. Also one of the schools of philosophy within Hinduism

Vedas: Ancient Hindu scriptures that were heard directly from God (shruti).

Vedic: Of the Vedas.

Vishnu: One of the forms of God. The aspect of God responsible for maintenance of the universe.

***Vishnu Purana*:** A scripture describing the glories of the Lord Vishnu.

***Viveka-cūḍāmaṇi*:** Literally, "The Jewel of Wisdom." A famous book by Sri Śaṅkarācārya introducing the Advaita Vedanta philosophy.

Vraja: The area around Vrindavana, India.

Vrindavana: The village in India where Sri Krishna spent his childhood and where his early pastimes took place.

Vyāsadeva: Compiler of the Vedas and most of the Puranas. The literary incarnation of Lord Vishnu.

Y

***Yoga Sutra*:** A fundamental text of raja yoga, compiled by Patañjali Maharishi.

Yogi: A practitioner of yoga.

Sanskrit pronunciation guide

The Sanskrit Alphabet

Vowels

अ *a* आ *ā* इ *i* ई *ī* उ *u* ऊ *ū*
ऋ *ṛ* ॠ *ṝ* ऌ *ḷ* ए *e* ऐ *ai* ओ *o* औ *au* अं *aṁ* अः *aḥ*

Consonants

Gutturals	क *ka*	ख *kha*	ग *ga*	घ *gha*	ङ ṅa
Palatals	च *ca*	छ *cha*	ज *ja*	झ *jha*	ञ ña
Cerebrals	ट *ṭa*	ठ *ṭha*	ड *ḍa*	ढ *ḍha*	ण ṇa
Dentals	त *ta*	थ *tha*	द *da*	ध *dha*	न na
Labials	प *pa*	फ *pha*	ब *ba*	भ *bha*	म ma
Semivowels	य *ya*	र *ra*	ल *la*	व *va*	
Sibilants	श *śa*	ष *ṣa*	स *sa*		
Aspirates	ह *ha*				

Pronunciation

Vowels

Sanskrit letter	Transliteration	Sounds like
अ	*a*	but
आ	*ā*	father
इ	*i*	fit, if, lily
ई	*ī*	fee, police
उ	*u*	put
ऊ	*ū*	boot, rule, rude
ऋ	*ṛ*	(between ri and
ru,		as in the name Krishna)
ॠ	*ṝ*	(between ri and ru) crucial
ऌ	*ḷ*	(similar to lr)
ए	*e*	made
ऐ	*ai*	bite, aisle
ओ	*o*	oh
औ	*au*	found, house

Consonants

Gutturals

(back of the throat)

Sanskrit letter	Transliteration	Sounds like
क	*ka*	kill, seek, kite
ख	*kha*	Eckhart
ग	*ga*	get, dog, give
घ	*gha*	log-hut
ङ	*ṅa*	sing, king, sink

Palatals

(tip of the tongue touches the roof of the mouth)

Sanskrit letter	Transliteration	Sounds like
च	*ca*	chicken
छ	*cha*	catch him
ज	*ja*	joy, jump
झ	*jha*	hedgehog
ञ	*ña*	canyon

Cerebrals

(tip of the tongue against the front part of the roof of the mouth)

Sanskrit letter	Transliteration	Sounds like
ट	*ṭa*	true, tub
ठ	*ṭha*	anthill
ड	*ḍa*	dove, drum, doctor
ढ	*ḍha*	red-hot
ण	*ṇa*	under

Dentals

(tip of the tongue against the teeth)

Sanskrit letter	Transliteration	Sounds like
त	*ta*	(between t and th) water
थ	*tha*	lighthearted
द	*da*	(between d and th) dice, then
ध	*dha*	adhere
न	*na*	not, nut

Labials

(lips together, the tongue is not used)

Sanskrit letter	Transliteration	Sounds like
प	*pa*	pine, put, sip
फ	*pha*	uphill
ब	*ba*	bird, bear, rub
भ	*bha*	abhor
म	*ma*	mother, map

Semivowels

Sanskrit letter	Transliteration	Sounds like
य	*ya*	yet, loyal, yes
र	*ra*	red, year
ल	*la*	lull, lead
व	*va*	(between v and w) ivy, vine

Sibilants

Sanskrit letter	Transliteration	Sounds like
श	*śa*	sure
ष	*ṣa*	shrink, bush, show
स	*sa*	saint, sin, hiss

Aspirate

Sanskrit letter	Transliteration	Sounds like
ह	*ha*	hear, hit, home

Additional Sounds

Anusvāra

A nasal sound, written as a dot above and to the right of a Sanskrit letter.

Sanskrit letter	Transliteration	Sounds like
ं	*ṁ*	hum, tempt, pump

Visarga

A final aspirate sound, written as two dots after a Sanskrit letter.

Sanskrit letter	Transliteration	Sounds like
ः	*ḥ*	ha or hi
तः	*taḥ*	'ta-ha'
तीः	*tīḥ*	'tee-hi'

Prabhuji
H.H. Avadhūta Śrī Bhaktivedānta Yogācārya
Ramakrishnananda Bābājī Mahārāja

About Prabhuji

Prabhuji is a writer, painter, an *avadhūta*, the creator of Retroprogressive Yoga, and a realized spiritual master. In 2011, he chose to retire from society and lead the life of a hermit. Since then, his days have been spent in solitude, praying, writing, painting, and meditating in silence and contemplation.

Prabhuji is the sole disciple of H.D.G. Avadhūta Śrī Brahmānanda Bābājī Mahārāja, who in turn is one of the closest and most intimate disciples of H.D.G. Avadhūta Śrī Mastarāma Bābājī Mahārāja.

Prabhuji was appointed as the successor of the lineage by his master, who conferred upon him the responsibility of continuing the sacred *paramparā* of *avadhūtas*, officially appointing him as guru and ordering him to serve as Ācārya successor under the name H.H. Avadhūta Śrī Bhaktivedānta Yogācārya Ramakrishnananda Bābājī Mahārāja.

Prabhuji is also a disciple of H.D.G. Bhakti-kavi Atulānanda Ācārya Mahārāja, who is a direct disciple of H.D.G. A.C. Bhaktivedānta Swami Prabhupāda.

Prabhuji's Hinduism is so broad, universal, and pluralistic that at times, while living up to his title of *avadhūta*, his lively and fresh teachings transcend the boundaries of all philosophies and religions, even his own. His teachings promote critical thinking and lead us to question statements that are usually accepted as true. They do not defend absolute truths but invite us to evaluate and question our own convictions. The essence of his syncretic vision, Retroprogressive Yoga, is self-awareness and the recognition of consciousness. For him, awakening at the level of consciousness, or the transcendence of the egoic phenomenon, is the next step in humanity's evolution.

Prabhuji was born on March 21, 1958, in Santiago, the capital of the Republic of Chile. When he was eight years old, he had a mystical experience that motivated his search for the Truth, or the Ultimate Reality. This transformed his life into an authentic inner and outer pilgrimage. He has completely devoted his life to deepening the early transformative experience that marked the beginning of his process of retroevolution. He has dedicated more than fifty years to the exploration and practice of different religions, philosophies, paths of liberation, and spiritual disciplines. He has absorbed the teachings of great yogis, pastors, rabbis, monks, gurus, philosophers, sages, and saints whom he personally visited during years of searching. He has lived in many places and traveled the world thirsting for Truth.

From an early age, Prabhuji noticed that the educational system prevented him from devoting himself to what was really important: learning about himself. Despite his parents' insistence, he stopped attending conventional school at the age of 11 and engaged in autodidactic formation. Over time, he would become a serious critic of the current educational system.

Prabhuji is a recognized authority on Eastern wisdom. He is known for his erudition in the *Vaidika* and *Tāntrika* aspects of Hinduism and all branches of yoga (*jñāna*, *karma*, *bhakti*, *haṭha*, *rāja*, *kuṇḍalinī*, *tantra*, *mantra*, and others). He has an inclusive attitude toward all religions and is intimately familiar with Judaism, Christianity, Buddhism, Sufism, Taoism, Sikhism, Jainism, Shintoism, Bahaism, and the Mapuche religion, among others. He learned about the Druze religion directly from the scholars Salach Abbas and Kamil Shchadi.

Prabhuji studied Christian theology in depth with H.H. Monsignor Iván Larraín Eyzaguirre at the Veracruz Church in Santiago de Chile and with Mr. Héctor Muñoz, who holds a degree in theology from the Universidad Católica de la Santísima Concepción.

His curiosity for Western thought led him to venture into the field of philosophy in all its different branches. He specialized in Transcendental Phenomenology and the Phenomenology of Religion. He had the privilege of studying intensively for several years with his uncle Jorge Balazs, philosopher, researcher, writer, and author of *The Golden Deer*. He studied privately for a few years with Dr. Jonathan Ramos, a renowned philosopher, historian, and university professor graduated from the Catholic University of Salta, Argentina. He also studied with Dr. Alejandro Cavallazzi Sánchez, who holds an undergraduate degree in philosophy from the Universidad Panamericana, a master's degree in philosophy from the Universidad Iberoamericana, and a doctorate in philosophy from the Universidad Nacional Autónoma de México (UNAM).

Prabhuji holds a doctorate in Vaishnava philosophy from the respected Jiva Institute in Vrindavan, India, and a doctorate in yogic philosophy from the Yoga Samskrutum University.

His profound studies, his masters' blessings, his research into the sacred scriptures, and his vast teaching experience have earned him international recognition in the field of religion and spirituality.

His spiritual search led him to study with masters of diverse traditions and travel far from his native Chile to places as distant as Israel, India, and the USA. Prabhuji studied Hebrew and Sanskrit to deepen his understanding of the holy scriptures. He also studied Pali at the Oxford Centre for Buddhist Studies. Furthermore, he learned ancient Latin and Greek from Javier Álvarez, who holds a degree in Classical Philology from the Sevilla University.

His father, Yosef Har-Zion ZT"L, grew up under strict discipline because he was the son of a senior police sergeant. As a reaction to this upbringing, Yosef decided to raise his own children with complete freedom and unconditional love. Prabhuji grew up without any pressure. During his early years, his father showed his son the same love regardless of his successes or failures at school. When Prabhuji decided to drop out of school to devote himself to his inner quest, his family accepted his decision with deep respect. From the time his son was ten years old, Yosef talked to him about Hebrew spirituality and

Western philosophy. They engaged in conversations about philosophy and religion for days on end and late into the night. Yosef supported him in whatever he wanted to do in his life and his search for Truth. Prabhuji was the authentic project of freedom and unconditional love of his father.

At an early age and on his own initiative, Prabhuji began to practice karate and study philosophy and religion. During his adolescence, no one interfered with his decisions. At the age of 15, he established a deep, intimate, and long friendship with the famous Uruguayan writer and poet Blanca Luz Brum, who was his neighbor on Merced Street in Santiago de Chile. He traveled throughout Chile in search of wise and interesting people to learn from. In southern Chile, he met machis who taught him about the rich Mapuche spirituality and shamanism.

Two great masters contributed to Prabhuji's retroprogressive process. In 1976, he met his first guru, H.D.G Bhakti-kavi Atulānanda Ācārya Swami, whom he would call Gurudeva. In those days, Gurudeva was a young *brahmacārī* who held the position of president of the ISKCON temple at Eyzaguirre 2404, Puente Alto, Santiago, Chile. Years later, he gave Prabhuji first initiation, Brahminical initiation, and, finally, he initiated Prabhuji into the sacred order of renunciation called *sannyāsa* within the Brahma Gauḍīya Saṁpradāya. Gurudeva connected him to the devotion to Kṛṣṇa. He imparted to him the wisdom of bhakti yoga and instructed him in the practice of the *māhā-mantra* and the study of the holy scriptures.

In 1996, Prabhuji met his second guru, H.D.G. Avadhūta Śrī Brahmānanda Bābājī Mahārāja, in Rishikesh, India. Guru Mahārāja, as Prabhuji called him, revealed that his own master, H.D.G. Avadhūta Śrī Mastarāma Bābājī Mahārāja, had told him years before he died that a person would come from the West and request to be his disciple. He commanded him to accept only that particular seeker. When he asked how he would identify this person, Mastarāma Bābājī replied, "You will recognize him by his eyes. You must accept him because he will be the continuation of the lineage."

From his first meeting with young Prabhuji, Guru Mahārāja recognized him and officially initiated him into the *māhā-mantra*. For Prabhuji, this initiation marked the beginning of the most intense and mature stage his retroprogressive process. Under the guidance of Guru Mahārāja, he studied Advaita Vedanta and deepened his meditation.

Guru Mahārāja guided Prabhuji on his first steps toward the sacred level of *avadhūta*. In March 2011, H.D.G. Avadhūta Śrī Brahmānanda Bābājī Mahārāja ordered Prabhuji, on behalf of his own master, to accept the responsibility of continuing the lineage of *avadhūtas*. With this title, Prabhuji is the official representative of the line of this disciplic succession for the present generation. Besides his *dikṣā-gurus*, Prabhuji studied with important spiritual and religious personalities, such as H.H. Swami Dayananda Sarasvatī, H.H. Swami Viṣṇu Devānanda Sarasvatī, H.H. Swami Jyotirmayānanda Sarasvatī, H.H. Swami Pratyagbodhānanda, H.H. Swami

Swahananda of the Ramakrishna Mission, and H.H. Swami Viditātmānanda of the Arsha Vidya Gurukulam. The wisdom of tantra was awakened in Prabhuji by H.G. Mātājī Rīnā Śarmā in India.

Prabhuji wanted to confirm his *sannyāsa* initiation in an Advaita Vedanta lineage. His *sannyāsa-dīkṣā* was confirmed by H.H. Swami Jyotirmayānanda Sarasvatī, founder of the Yoga Research Foundation and disciple of H.H. Swami Śivānanda Sarasvatī of Rishikesh.

In 1984, he learned and began to practice Maharishi Mahesh Yogi's Transcendental Meditation technique. In 1988, he took the *kriyā-yoga* course on Paramahaṁsa Yogananda. After two years, he was officially initiated into the technique of *kriyā-yoga* by the Self-Realization Fellowship.

In Vrindavan, studied the bhakti yoga path in depth with H.H. Narahari Dāsa Bābājī Mahārāja, disciple of H.H. Nityananda Dāsa Bābājī Mahārāja of Vraja.

He also studied bhakti yoga with various disciples of His Divine Grace A.C. Bhaktivedānta Swami Prabhupāda: H.H. Kapīndra Swami, H.H. Paramadvaiti Mahārāja, H.H. Jagajīvana Dāsa, H.H. Tamāla Kṛṣṇa Gosvāmī, H.H. Bhagavān Dāsa Mahārāja, and H.H. Kīrtanānanda Swami, among others.

Prabhuji has been honored with various titles and diplomas by many leaders of prestigious religious and spiritual institutions in India. He was given the honorable title *Kṛṣṇa Bhakta* by H.H. Swami Viṣṇu Devānanda (the only title of Bhakti Yoga given by Swami Viṣṇu), disciple of H.H. Swami Śivānanda Sarasvatī and the founder of the Sivananda Organization. He was given the title

Bhaktivedānta by H.H. B.A. Paramadvaiti Mahārāja, the founder of Vrinda. He was given the title *Yogācārya* by H.H. Swami Viṣṇu Devānanda, the Paramanand Institute of Yoga Sciences and Research of Indore, India, the International Yoga Federation, the Indian Association of Yoga, and the Shri Shankarananda Yogashram of Mysore, India. He received the respectable title *Śrī Śrī Rādhā Śyam Sunder Pāda-Padma Bhakta Śiromaṇi* directly from H.H. Satyanārāyaṇa Dāsa Bābājī Mahant of the Chatu Vaiṣṇava Saṁpradāya.

Prabhuji spent more than forty years studying hatha yoga with prestigious masters in classical and traditional yoga, such as H.H. Bapuji, H.H. Swami Viṣṇu Devānanda Sarasvatī, H.H. Swami Jyotirmayānanda Sarasvatī, H.H. Swami Satchidananda Sarasvatī, H.H. Swami Vignanananda Sarasvatī, and Śrī Madana-mohana.

He attended several systematic hatha yoga teacher training courses at prestigious institutions until he achieved the level of Master Ācārya. He has completed studies at the following institutions: the Sivananda Yoga Vedanta, the Ananda Ashram, the Yoga Research Foundation, the Integral Yoga Academy, the Patanjala Yoga Kendra, the Ma Yoga Shakti International Mission, the Prana Yoga Organization, the Rishikesh Yoga Peeth, the Swami Sivananda Yoga Research Center, and the Swami Sivananda Yogasana Research Center.

Prabhuji is a member of the Indian Association of Yoga, Yoga Alliance ERYT 500 and YACEP, the International Association of Yoga Therapists, and the International Yoga Federation. In 2014, the International Yoga Federation honored him with the position of Honorary Member of the World Yoga Council.

His interest in the complex anatomy of the human body led him to study chiropractic at the prestigious Institute of Health of the Back and Extremities in Tel Aviv, Israel. In 1993, he received a diploma from Dr. Sheinerman, the founder and director of the institute. Later, he earned a massage therapy diploma at the Academy of Western Galilee. The knowledge he acquired in this field deepened his understanding of hatha yoga and contributed to the creation of his own method.

Retroprogressive Hatha Yoga is the result of Prabhuji's efforts to improve his practice and teaching methods. It is a system based especially on the teachings of his gurus and the sacred scriptures. Prabhuji has systematized various traditional yoga techniques to create a methodology suitable for Western audiences. Retroprogressive Yoga aims to experience our true nature. It promotes balance, health, and flexibility through proper diet, cleansing techniques, preparations (*āyojanas*), sequences (*vinyāsas*), postures (*asanas*), breathing exercises (*prāṇayama*), relaxation (*śavāsana*), meditation (*dhyāna*), and exercises with locks (*bandhas*) and seals (*mudras*) to direct and empower *prāṇa*.

Since his childhood and throughout his life, Prabhuji has been an enthusiastic admirer, student, and practitioner of classic karate-do. From the age of 13, he studied different styles in Chile, such as kenpo and kung-fu, but specialized in the most traditional Japanese style of shotokan. He received the rank of black belt (third dan) from Shihan

Kenneth Funakoshi (ninth dan). He also learned from Sensei Takahashi (seventh dan) and practiced Shorin Ryu style with Sensei Enrique Daniel Welcher (seventh dan), who granted him the rank of black belt (second dan). Through karate-do, he delved into Buddhism and gained additional knowledge about the physics of motion. Prabhuji is a member of Funakoshi's Shotokan Karate Association.

Prabhuji grew up in an artistic environment and his love of painting began to develop in his childhood. His father, the renowned Chilean painter Yosef Har-Zion ZT"L, motivated him to devote himself to art. He learned with the famous Chilean painter Marcelo Cuevas. Prabhuji's abstract paintings reflect the depths of the spirit.

Since he was a young boy, Prabhuji has been especially drawn to postal stamps, postcards, mailboxes, postal transportation systems, and all mail-related activities. He has taken every opportunity to visit post offices in different cities and countries. He has delved into the study of philately, the field of collecting, sorting, and studying postage stamps. This passion led him to become a professional philatelist, a stamp distributor authorized by the American Philatelic Society, and a member of the following societies: the Royal Philatelic Society London, the Royal Philatelic Society of Victoria, the United States Stamp Society, the Great Britain Philatelic Society, the American Philatelic Society, the Society of Israel Philatelists, the Society for Hungarian Philately, the National Philatelic Society UK, the Fort Orange Stamp Club, the American Stamp Dealers Association, the US Philatelic Classics Society, Filabras – Associação dos Filatelistas Brasileiros, and the Collectors Club of NYC.

Based on his extensive knowledge of philately, theology, and Eastern philosophy, Prabhuji created "Meditative Philately" or "Philatelic Yoga," a spiritual practice that uses philately as the basis for practicing attention, concentration, observation, and meditation. Meditative Philately is inspired by the ancient Hindu *maṇḍala* meditation and it can lead the practitioner to elevated states of consciousness, deep relaxation, and concentration that fosters the recognition of consciousness. Prabhuji wrote his thesis on this new type of yoga, "Meditative Philately," attracting the interest of the Indian academic community due to its innovative way of connecting meditation with different hobbies and activities. For this thesis, he was honored with a PhD in Yogic Philosophy from Yoga-Samskrutum University.

Prabhuji lived in Israel for many years, where he furthered his studies of Judaism. One of his main teachers and sources of inspiration was Rabbi Shalom Dov Lifshitz ZT"L, whom he met in 1997. This great saint guided him for several years on the intricate paths of the Torah and Chassidism. The two developed a very intimate relationship. Prabhuji studied the Talmud with Rabbi Raphael Rapaport Shlit"a (Ponovich), Chassidism with Rabbi Israel Lifshitz Shlit"a, and the Torah with Rabbi Daniel Sandler Shlit"a. Prabhuji is a great devotee of Rabbi Mordechai Eliyahu ZT"L, who personally blessed him.

Prabhuji visited the United States in 2000 and during his stay in New York, he realized that it was the most appropriate place to found a religious organization. He was particularly attracted by the pluralism and respectful attitude of American society toward freedom of religion. He was impressed by the deep respect of both the public and the government for religious minorities. After consulting his masters and requesting their blessings, Prabhuji relocated to the United States. In 2003, the Prabhuji Mission was born, a Hindu church aimed at preserving Prabhuji's universal and pluralistic vision of Hinduism and his Retroprogressive Yoga.

Although he did not seek to attract followers, for 15 years (1995–2010), Prabhuji considered the requests of a few people who approached him asking to become his monastic disciples. Those who chose to see Prabhuji as their spiritual master voluntarily accepted vows of poverty and life-long dedication to spiritual practice (*sadhāna*), religious devotion (*bhakti*), and selfless service (*seva*). Although Prabhuji no longer accepts new disciples, he continues to guide the small group of monastic disciples of the Ramakrishnananda Monastic Order that he founded.

In 2011, Prabhuji founded the Avadhutashram (monastery) in the Catskills Mountains in upstate New York, USA. The Avadhutashram is the headquarters of the Prabhuji Mission, his hermitage, and the residence of the monastic disciples of the Ramakrishnananda Monastic Order. The ashram organizes humanitarian projects such as the Prabhuji Food Distribution Program and the Prabhuji Toy Distribution Program. Prabhuji operates various humanitarian projects, inspired in his experience that serving the part is serving the Whole.

In January 2012, Prabhuji's health forced him to officially renounce managing the mission. Since then, he has lived in solitude, completely away from the public, writing and absorbed in contemplation. His message does not promote collective spirituality, but individual inner search.

Prabhuji has delegated the choice to his disciples between keeping his teachings exclusively within the monastic order or spreading his message for the public benefit. Upon the explicit request of his disciples, Prabhuji has agreed to have his books published and his lectures disseminated, as long as this does not compromise his privacy and his life as a hermit.

In 2022, Prabhuji founded the Institute of Retroprogressive Yoga. Here, his most senior disciples can systematically share Prabhuji's teachings and message through video conferences. The institute offers support and help for a deeper understanding of Prabhuji's teachings.

Prabhuji is a respected member of the American Philosophical Association, the American Association of Philosophy Teachers, the American Association of University Professors, the Southwestern Philosophical Society, the Authors Guild, the National Writers Union, PEN America, the International Writers Association, the National Association of Independent Writers and Editors, the National Writers Association, the Alliance Independent Authors, and the Independent Book Publishers Association.

Prabhuji's vast literary contribution includes books in Spanish, English, and Hebrew, for example, *Kundalini Yoga: The Power is in you*, *What is, as it is*, *Bhakti-Yoga: The Path of Love*, *Tantra: Liberation in the World*, *Experimenting with the Truth*, *Advaita Vedanta: Be the Self*, commentaries on the *Īśāvāsya Upanishad* and the *Diamond Sūtra*.

About the Prabhuji Mission

Prabhuji, H.H. Avadhūta Śrī Bhaktivedānta Yogācārya Ramakrishnananda Bābājī Mahārāja, founded the Prabhuji Mission in 2003, a Hindu church aimed at preserving his universal and pluralistic vision of Hinduism.

The main purpose of the mission is to preserve Prabhuji's teachings of Pūrvavyāpi-pragatiśīlaḥ Yoga, or Retroprogressive Yoga, which advocates for a global awakening of consciousness as the radical solution to humanity's problems.

The Prabhuji Mission operates a Hindu temple called Śrī Śrī Radha-Śyāmasundara Mandir, which offers worship and religious ceremonies to parishioners. The extensive library of the Retroprogressive Yoga Institute provides its teachers with abundant study materials to research the various theologies and philosophies explored by Prabhuji in his books and lectures. The Avadhutashram monastery educates monastic disciples on various aspects of Prabhuji's approach to Hinduism and offers them the opportunity to express devotion to God through devotional service by selflessly contributing their skills and training to the Mission's programs, such as the Prabhuji Food Distribution program, a weekly event in which dozens of families in need from Upstate New York receive fresh and nutritious food.

Service and glorification of the guru are fundamental spiritual principles in Hinduism. The Prabhuji Mission, as a traditional Hindu church, practices the millenary *guru-bhakti* tradition of reverence to the master. Some disciples and friends of the Prabhuji Mission, on their own initiative, help to preserve Prabhuji's legacy and his interfaith teachings for future generations by disseminating his books, videos of his internal talks, and websites.

About the Avadhutashram

The Avadhutashram (monastery) was founded by Prabhuji in the Catskills Mountains in upstate New York, USA. It is the headquarters of the Prabhuji Mission and the hermitage of H.H. Avadhūta Śrī Bhaktivedānta Yogācārya Ramakrishnananda Bābājī Mahārāja and his monastic disciples of the Ramakrishnananda Monastic Order.

The ideals of the Avadhutashram are love and selfless service, based on the universal vision that God is in everything and everyone. Its mission is to distribute spiritual books and organize humanitarian projects such as the Prabhuji Food Distribution Program and the Prabhuji Toy Distribution Program.

The Avadhutashram is not commercial and operates without soliciting donations. Its activities are funded by Prabhuji's Gifts, a non-profit company founded by Prabhuji, which sells esoteric items from different traditions that Prabhuji himself has used for spiritual practices during his evolutionary process. Its mission is to preserve and disseminate traditional religious, mystical, and ancestral crafts.

Avadhutashram
Round Top, NY, USA

The Retroprogressive Path

The Retroprogressive Path does not require you to be part of a group or a member of an organization, institution, society, congregation, club, or exclusive community. Living in a temple, monastery, or *āśram* is not mandatory, because it is not about a change of residence, but of consciousness. It does not urge you to believe, but to doubt. It does not demand you to accept something, but to explore, investigate, examine, inquire, and question everything. It does not suggest being what you should be but being what you really are.

The Retroprogressive Path supports freedom of expression but not proselytizing. This route does not promise answers to our questions but induces us to question our answers. It does not promise to be what we are not or to attain what we have not already achieved. It is a retro-evolutionary path of self-discovery that leads us from what we think we are to what we really are. It is not the only way, nor the best, the simplest, or the most direct. It is an involutionary process par excellence that shows what is obvious and undeniable but usually goes unnoticed: that which is simple, innocent, and natural. It is a path that begins and ends in you.

The Retroprogressive Path is a continuous revelation that expands eternally. It delves into consciousness from an ontological perspective, transcending all religion and spiritual paths. It is the discovery of diversity as a unique and inclusive reality. It is the encounter of consciousness with itself, aware of itself and its own reality. In fact, this path is a simple invitation to dance in the now, to love the present moment, and to celebrate our authenticity. It is an unconditional proposal to stop living as a victim of circumstance and to live as a passionate adventurer. It is a call to return to the place we have never left, without offering us anything we do not already possess or teaching us anything we do not already know. It is a call for an inner revolution and to enter the fire of life that only consumes dreams, illusions, and fantasies but does not touch what we are. It does not help us reach our desired goal, but instead prepares us for the unexpected miracle.

This path was nurtured over a lifetime dedicated to the search for Truth. It is a grateful offering to existence for what I have received. But remember, do not look for me. Look for yourself. It is not me you need, because you are the only one who really matters. This life is just a wonderful parenthesis in eternity to know and love. What you yearn for lies in you, here and now, as what you really are.

Your unconditional well-wisher,
Prabhuji

Prabhuji today

Prabhuji is retired from public life

Prabhuji is the sole disciple of H.D.G. Avadhūta Śrī Brahmānanda Bābājī Mahārāja, who is himself one of the closest and most intimate disciples of H.D.G. Avadhūta Śrī Mastarāma Bābājī Mahārāja.

Prabhuji was appointed as the successor of the lineage by his master, who conferred upon him the responsibility of continuing the sacred *paramparā* of *avadhūtas*, officially appointing him as guru and ordering him to serve as Ācārya successor under the name H.H. Avadhūta Śrī Bhaktivedānta Yogācārya Ramakrishnananda Bābājī Mahārāja.

Prabhuji is also a disciple of H.D.G. Bhakti-kavi Atulānanda Ācārya Mahārāja, who is a direct disciple of H.D.G. A.C. Bhaktivedānta Swami Prabhupāda.

In 2011, he chose to retire from society and lead the life of a hermit. Since then, his days have been spent in solitude, praying, writing, painting, and meditating in silence and contemplation. He no longer participates in *sat-saṅgs*, lectures, gatherings, meetings, retreats, seminars, study groups, or courses. We ask everyone to respect his privacy and do not try to contact him by any means for gatherings, meetings, interviews, blessings, *śaktipāta*, initiations, or personal visits.

Prabhuji's teachings

As an *avadhūta* and a realized spiritual master, Prabhuji has always appreciated the essence and spiritual wisdom of a wide variety of religious practices from around the world. He does not consider himself a member or representative of any particular religion. Although many see him as an enlightened being, Prabhuji has no intention of presenting himself as a preacher, guide, coach, content creator, influencer, preceptor, mentor, counselor, consultant, monitor, tutor, teacher, instructor, educator, enlightener, pedagogue, evangelist, rabbi, *posek halacha*, healer, therapist, satsangist, psychic, leader, medium, savior, or guru. In fact, Prabhuji believes spirituality is an individual, solitary, personal, private, and intimate search. It is not a collective endeavor to be undertaken through social, organized, institutional, or community religiosity.

To that end, Prabhuji does not proselytize or preach, nor does he try to persuade, convince, or make anyone change their perspective, philosophy, or religion. Others may find his insights valuable and apply them wholly or in part to their own development, but Prabhuji's teachings are not meant to be seen as personal advice, counseling, guidance, self-help methods, or techniques for spiritual, physical, emotional, or psychological development. His teachings do not promise solutions to life's spiritual, material, financial, psychological, emotional, romantic, family, social, or physical problems. Prabhuji does not offer miracles, mystical experiences, astral journeys, healings, connections with spirits, supernatural powers, or spiritual salvation.

Although he did not seek to attract followers, for 15 years (1995–2010), Prabhuji considered the requests of a few people who approached him asking to become his monastic disciples Those who chose to see Prabhuji as their spiritual master voluntarily accepted vows of poverty and life-long dedication to spiritual practice (*sādhanā*), religious devotion (*bhakti*), and selfless service (*seva*). Prabhuji no longer accepts new disciples, but he continues to guide the small group of veteran disciples of the Ramakrishnananda Monastic Order that he founded.

Public services

Even though the monastery does not accept new residents, volunteers, donations, collaborations, or sponsorships, the public is invited to participate in daily religious services and devotional festivals at the Śrī Śrī Radha-Śyāmasundara temple.

Titles by Prabhuji

What is, as it is: Satsangs with Prabhuji (English)
ISBN-13: 978-1-945894-26-8
Lo que es, tal como es: Satsangas con Prabhuji (Spanish)
ISBN-13: 978-1-945894-27-5
Russian: ISBN-13: 978-1-945894-18-3

Kundalini yoga: The power is in you (English)
ISBN-13: 978-1-945894-30-5
Kundalini yoga: El poder está en ti (Spanish)
ISBN-13: 978-1-945894-31-2

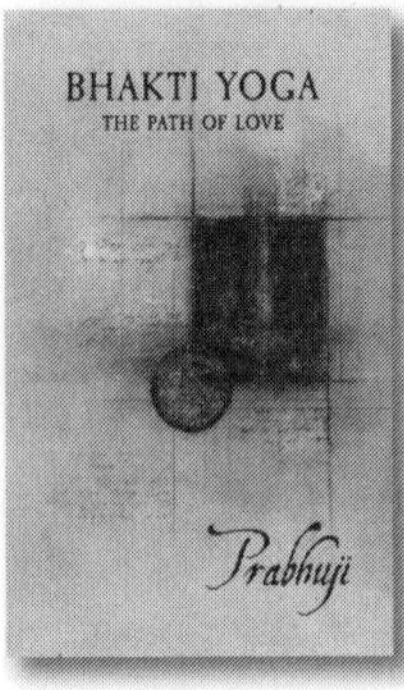

Bhakti yoga: The path of love (English)
ISBN-13: 978-1-945894-28-2
Bhakti-yoga: El sendero del amor (Spanish)
ISBN-13: 978-1-945894-29-9

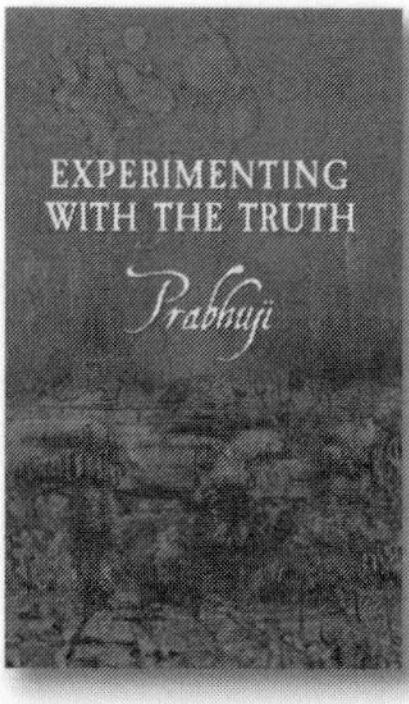

Experimenting with the Truth (English)
ISBN-13: 978-1-945894-32-9
Experimentando con la Verdad (Spanish)
ISBN-13: 978-1-945894-33-6

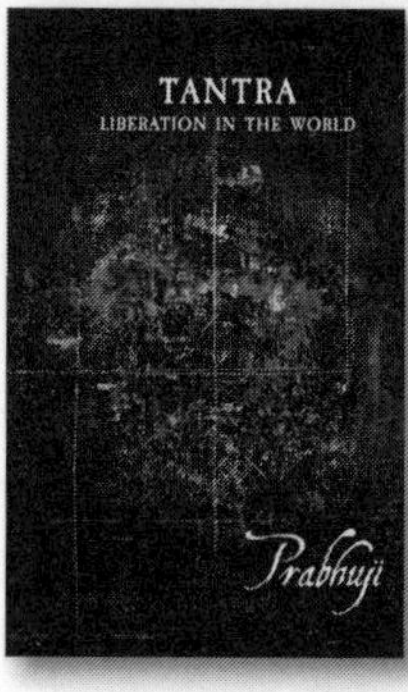

Tantra: Liberation in the world (English)
ISBN-13: 978-1-945894-36-7
Tantra: La liberación en el mundo (Spanish)
ISBN-13: 978-1-945894-37-4

Advaita Vedanta: Being the Self (English)
ISBN-13: 978-1-945894-34-3
Advaita Vedanta: Ser el Ser (Spanish)
ISBN-13: 978-1-945894-35-0

Īśāvāsya Upanishad
commented by Prabhuji
(English)
ISBN-13: 978-1-945894-38-1
Īśāvāsya Upaniṣad
comentado por Prabhuji
(Spanish)
ISBN-13: 978-1-945894-40-4

The Diamond Sūtra
commented by Prabhuji
(English)
ISBN-13: 978-1-945894-51-0
El Sūtra del Diamante
comentado por Prabhuji
(Spanish)
ISBN-13: 978-1-945894-54-1

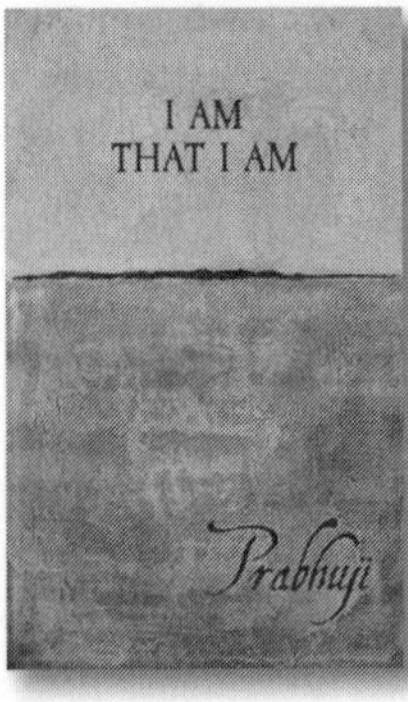

I am that I am
(English)
ISBN-13: 978-1-945894-45-9
Soy el que soy
(Spanish)
ISBN-13: 978-1-945894-48-0